Francesco Hayez:
85 Paintings

I0477301

By Maria Tsaneva

First Edition

*****

Foreword

Francesco Hayez (1791 – 1881) was an Italian painter and leading artist of Romanticism in mid-19th-century. His output spanned both historic paintings, including those that would have appealed to the patriotic sensibility of his patrons. Others reflect the desire to accompany a Neoclassic style to grand themes, either from biblical or classical literature. He also painted scenes from theatrical presentations of his day. Conspicuously lacking from his output, however, are altarpieces intended for devotional display. However, after the Napoleonic invasions deconsecrated many churches and convents in Northern Italy, the region was not lacking for religious artworks that were removed either to museums or concentrated in the remaining active religious institutions. Corrado Ricci describes him as starting as a classicist but then evolving to a style of emotional tumult.

His portraits have the intensity seen with Ingres and the Nazarene movement. Often sitting, the subjects dress in austere, often black and white clothing, with little to no accoutrements. While he did complete portraits for the nobility, other subjects are artists and musicians. Late in his career, he is known to have worked using photographs.

One of his favorite themes was a semi-clothed female. Often they were, like his Odalisque, evocative of oriental themes, which had been a favorite topic of Romantic painters. The depictions of harems and their women allowed them the ability to paint scenes not acceptable in their society. Even his Mary Magdalene has more sensuality than religious fervor.

Among his works, his painting The Kiss was considered among his best work by contemporaries, and has only gained in esteem since then. The anonymous, unaffected gesture of the couple does not require knowledge of myth or literature to interpret, and appeals to a modern gaze.

Assessment of the career of Hayez is complicated by the fact that he often did not sign or date his works. Often the date indicated from the evidence is that at which the work was acquired or sold, not of its creation. Moreover he often painted the same compositions several times with minimal variations, or even with no variation. His early works show the influence of his later work participates in the Classical revival.

Francesco Hayez lived long and was prolific. He came from a relatively poor family from Venice. His father was of French origin while his mother, Chiara Torcella, was from Murano. The child Francesco, youngest of five sons, was brought up by his mother's sister, who had married Giovanni Binasco, a well-off shipowner and collector of art. From childhood he showed a predisposition for drawing, so his uncle apprenticed him to an art restorer. Later he became a student of the painter Francesco Maggiotto with whom he continued his studies for three years. He was admitted to the painting course of the New Academy of Fine Arts in 1806, where he studied under Teodoro Matteini. In 1809 he won a competition from the Academy of Venice for one year of study at the Accademia di San Luca in Rome. He remained in Rome until 1814, and then moved to Naples where he was commissioned by Joachim Murat to paint a major work depicting Ulysses at the court of Alcinous. In the mid-1830s he attended the "Salotto Maffei" salon in Milan, hosted by Clara Maffei, and he was still in Milan in 1850 when he was appointed director of the Academy of Brera there.

Paintings

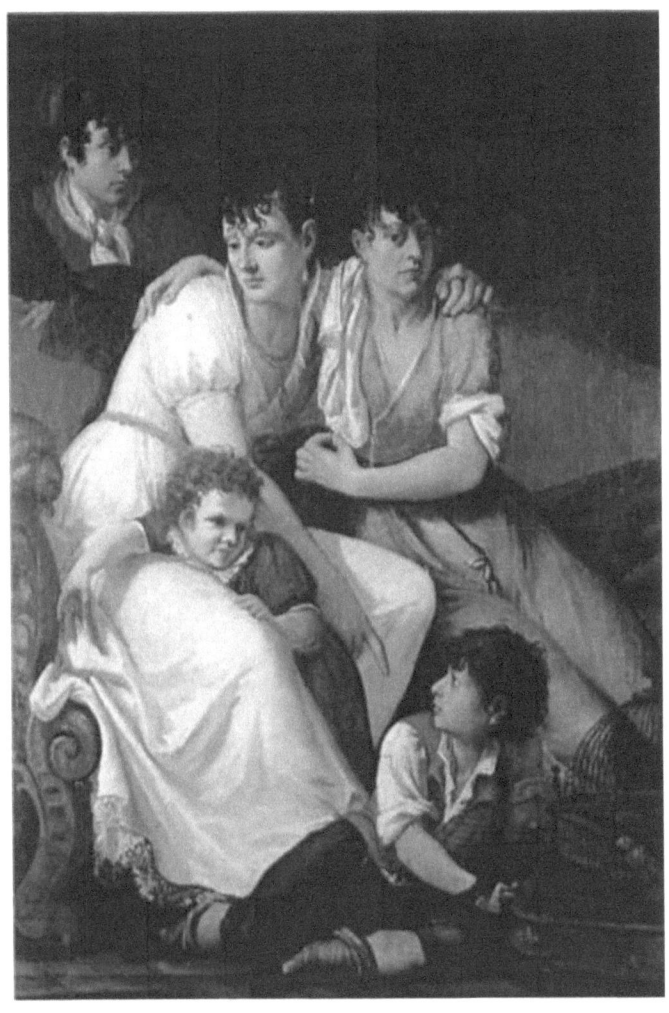

Family portrait, 1807, Oil on canvas

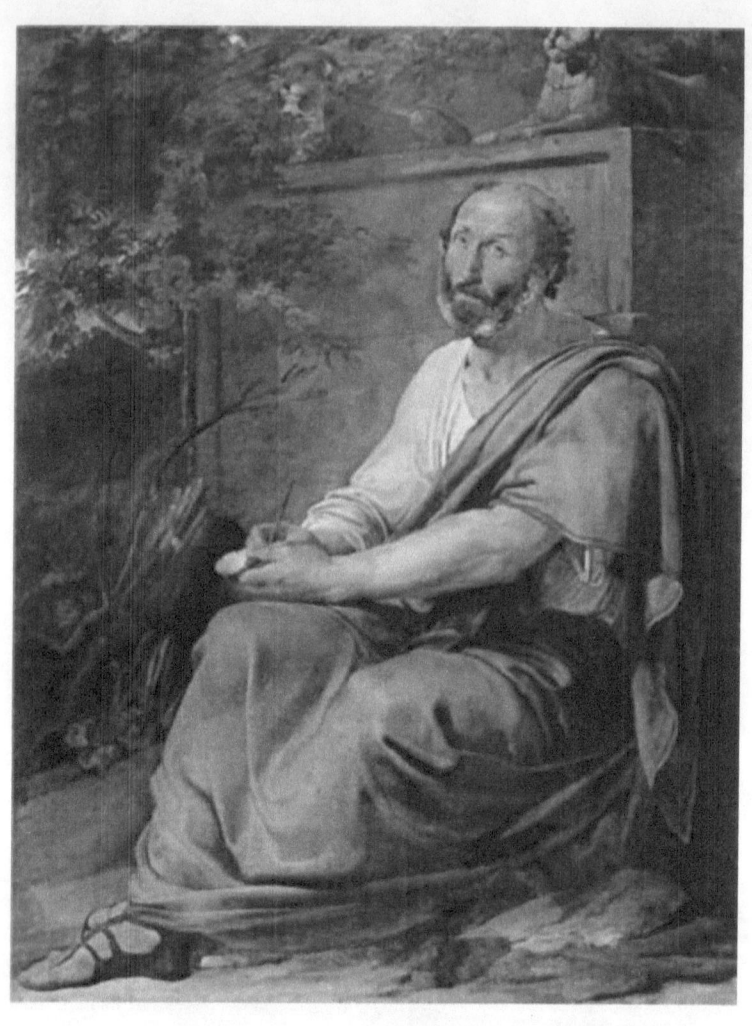

Aristoteles, 1811, Oil on canvas

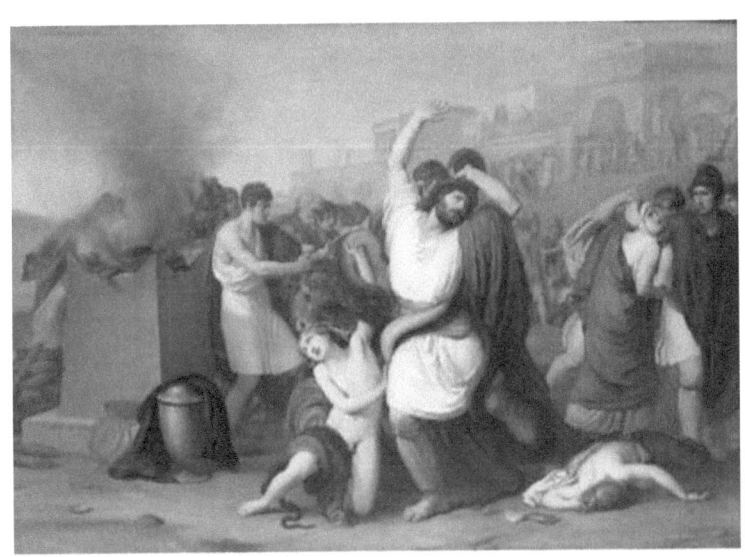

Laocoon, 1812, Oil on canvas

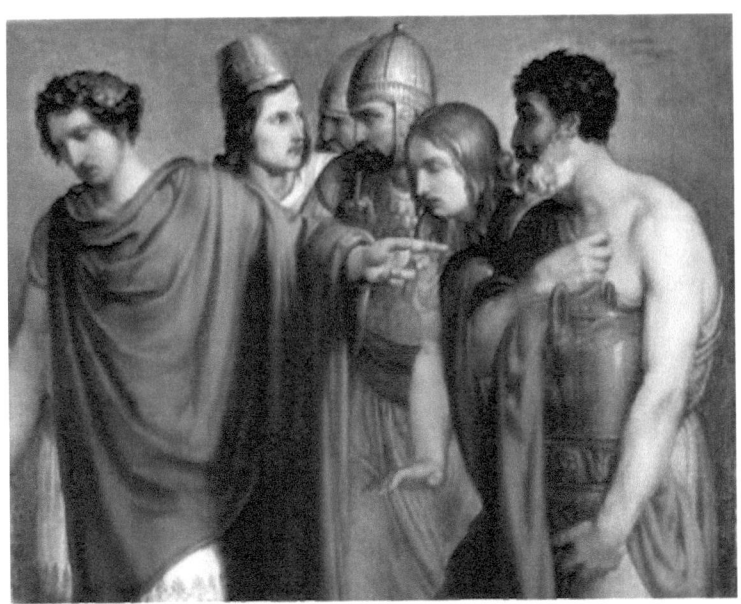

The Death of Abradates, 1813, Oil on canvas

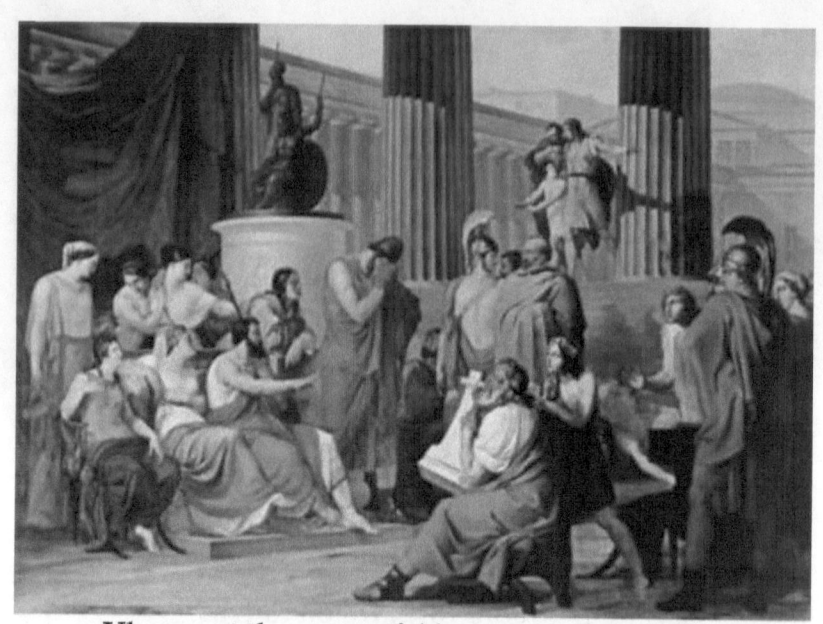

Ulysses at the court of Alcinous, c.1815, Oil on canvas

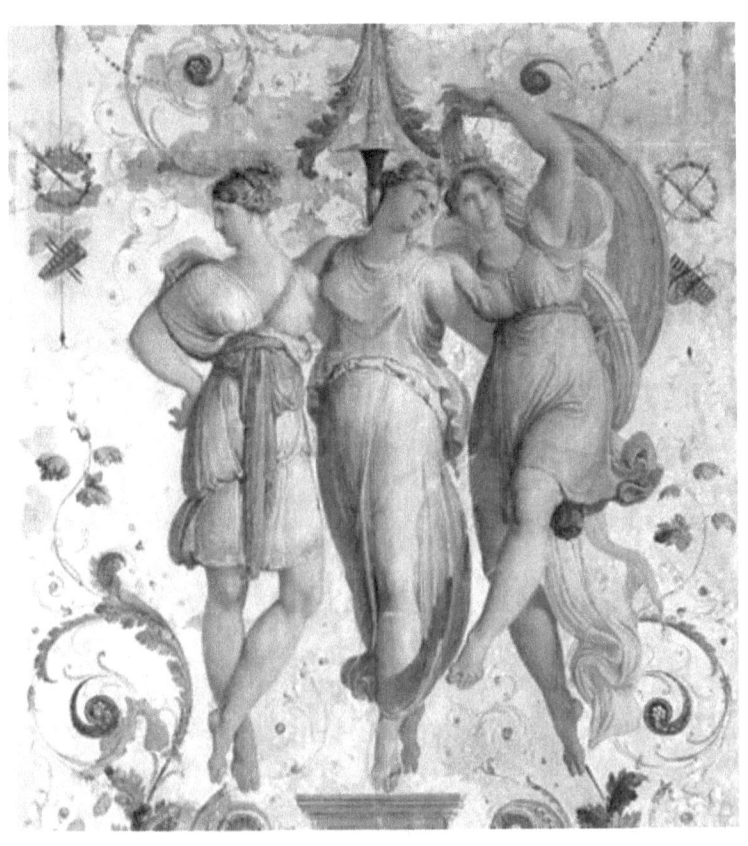

Wall Decoration (detail), 1817, Tempera on wall

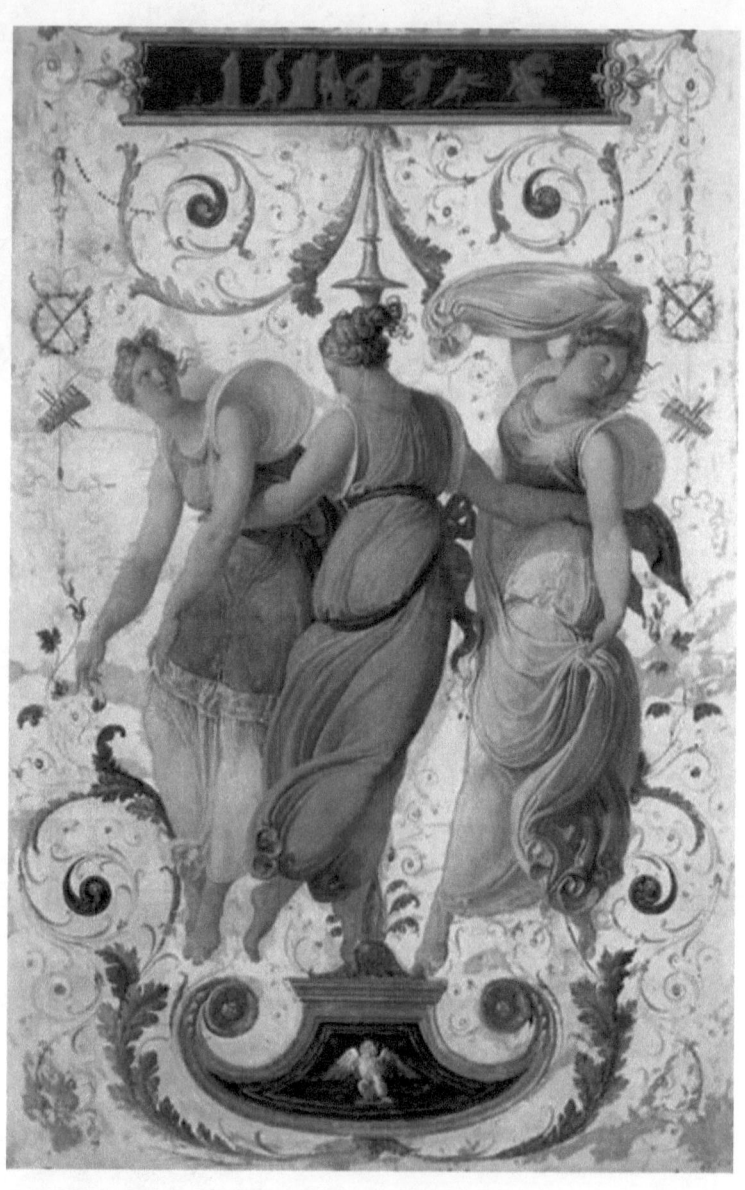

Wall Decoration (detail), 1817, Tempera on wall

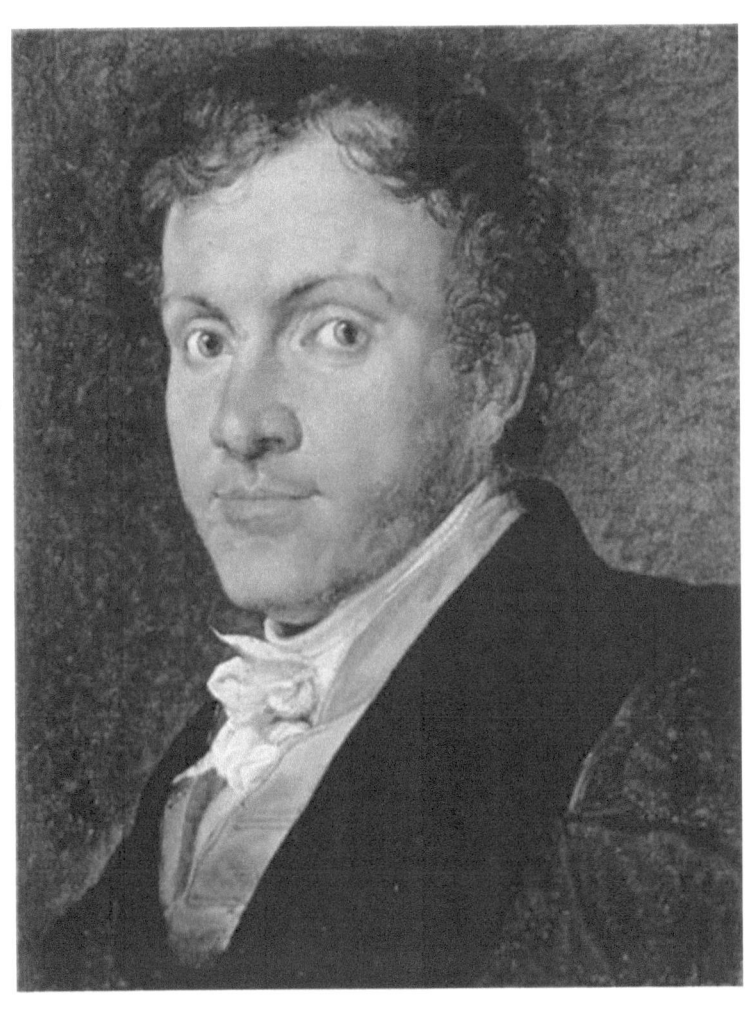

Portrait of Giuseppe Roberti, 1819, Oil on canvas

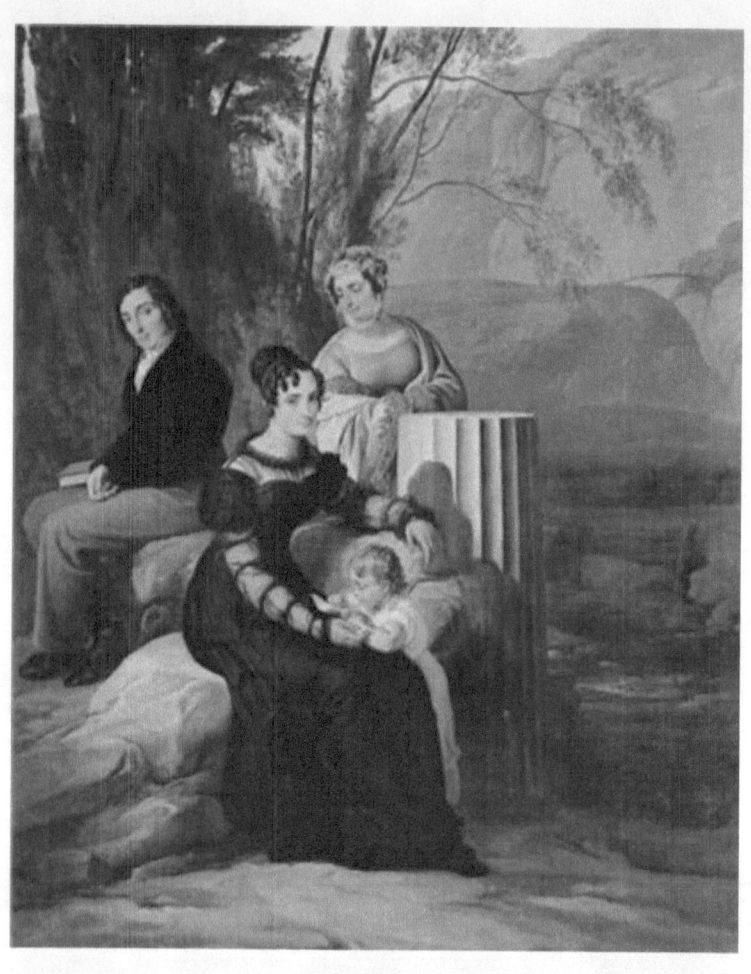

Portrait of Familie Stampa di Soncino, c.1822, Oil on canvas

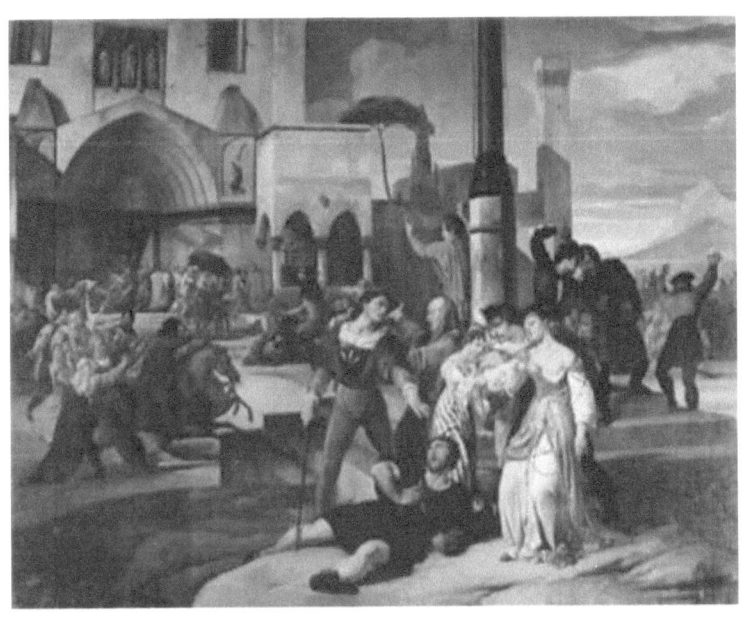

Sicilian evenings painting series, Scene 1, c.1822, Oil on canvas

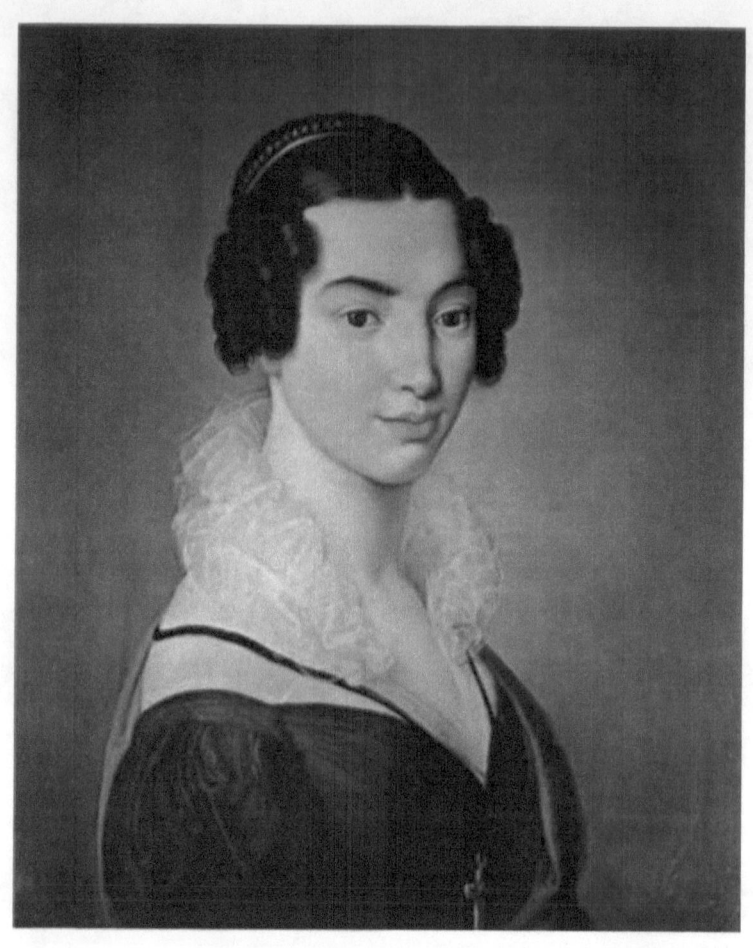

Portrait of Antoniet Vitali Sola, 1823, Oil on canvas

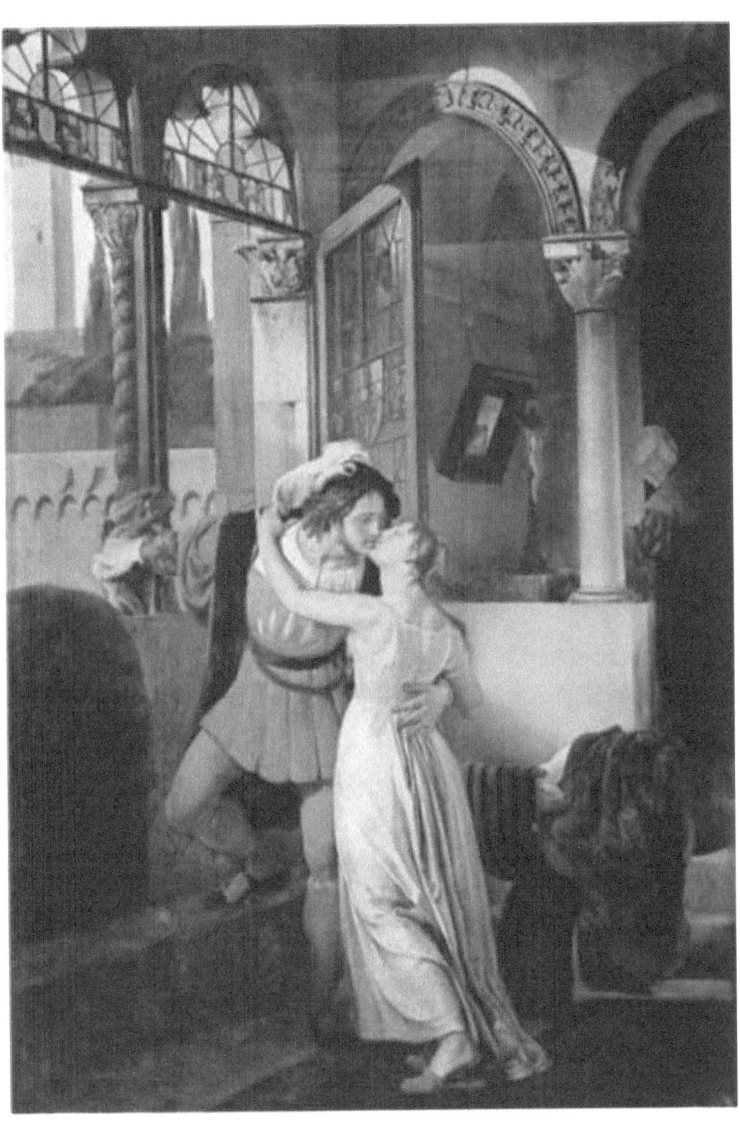

The last kiss of Romeo and Juliet, 1823, Oil on canvas

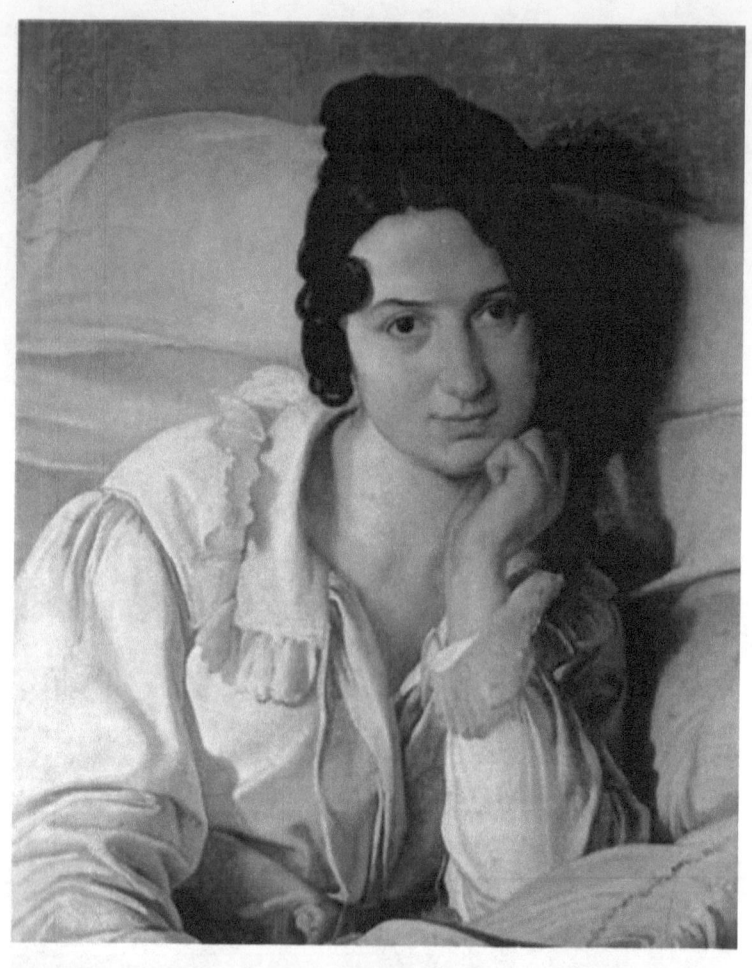

Carolina Zucchi (La Malata), 1825, Oil on canvas

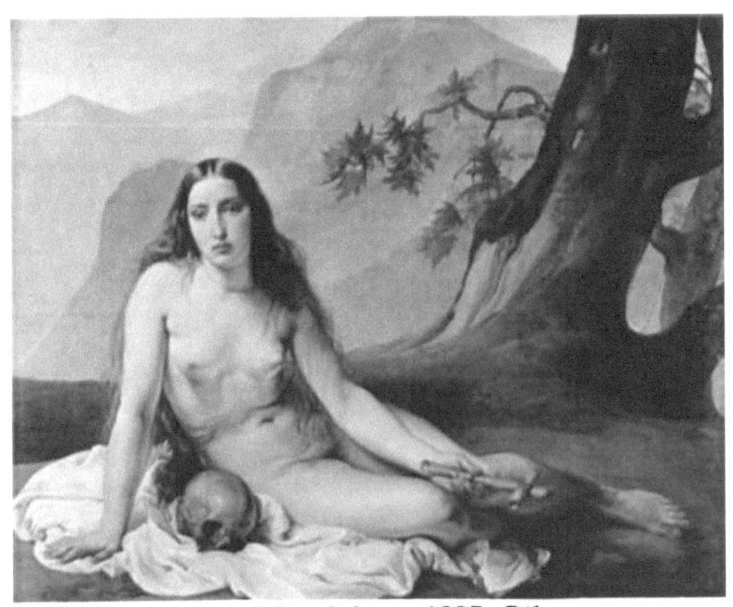

Penitent Mary Magdalene, 1825, Oil on canvas

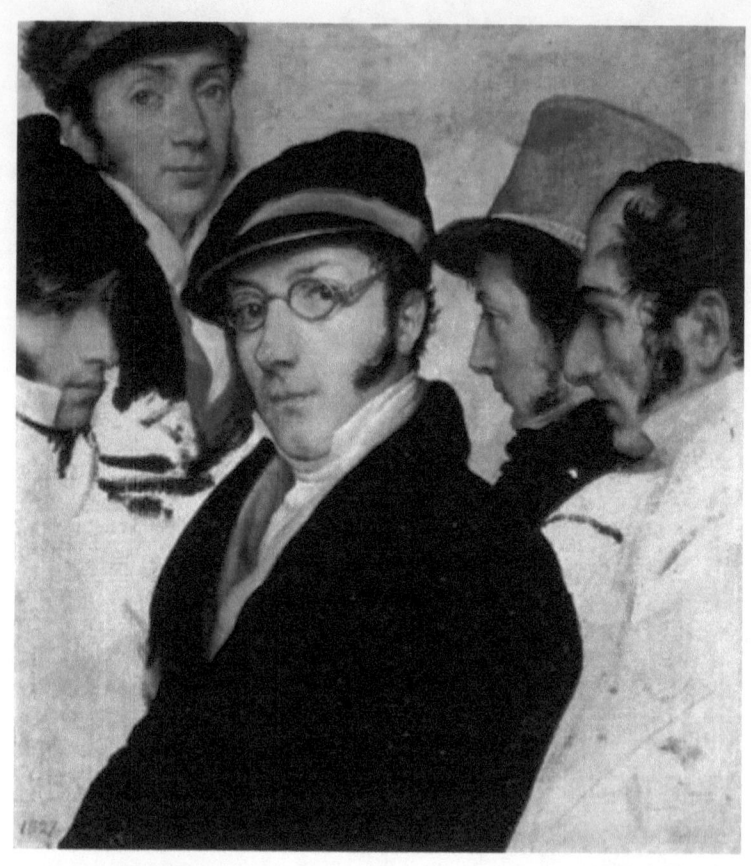

Self Portrait in a Group of Friends, c.1825, Oil on canvas

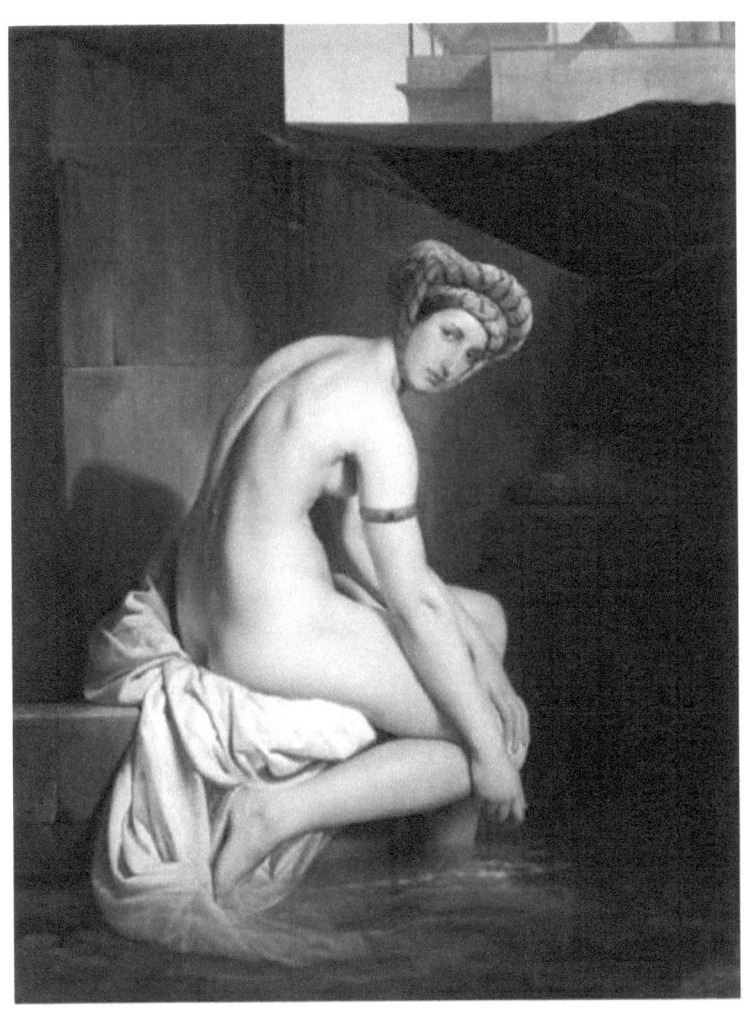

Bathsheba, c.1827, Oil on canvas

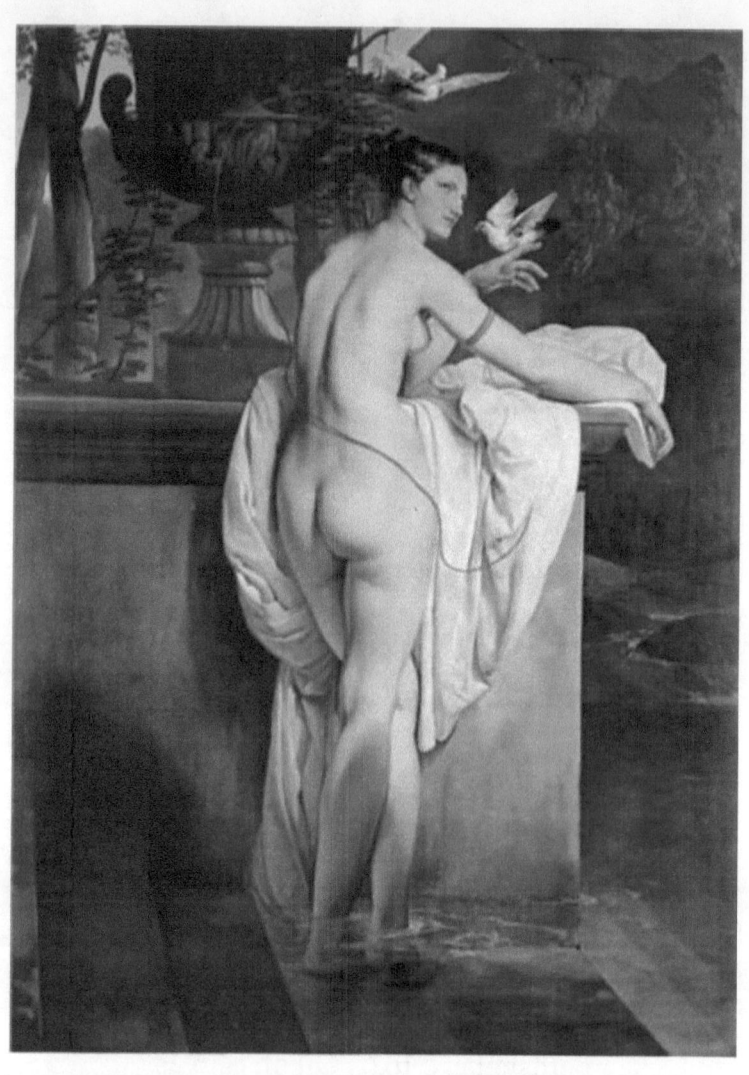

Ballerina Carlotta Chabert as Venus, 1830, Oil on canvas

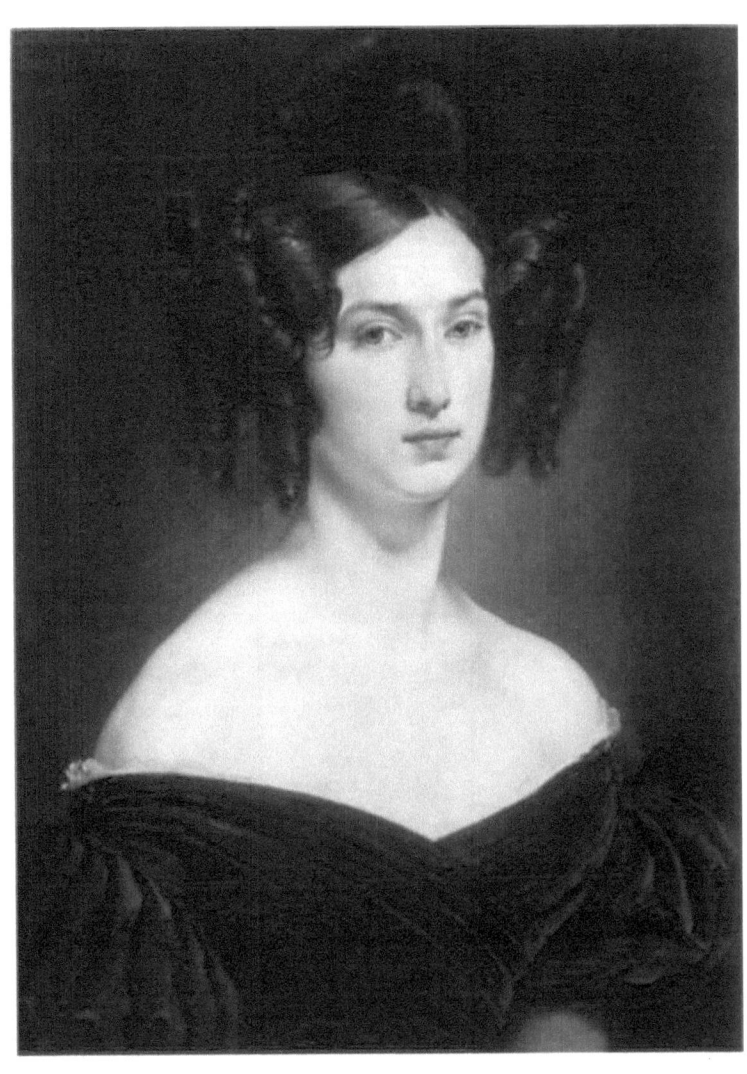

Portrait of Countess Luigia Douglas Scotti d'Adda,
1830, Oil on canvas

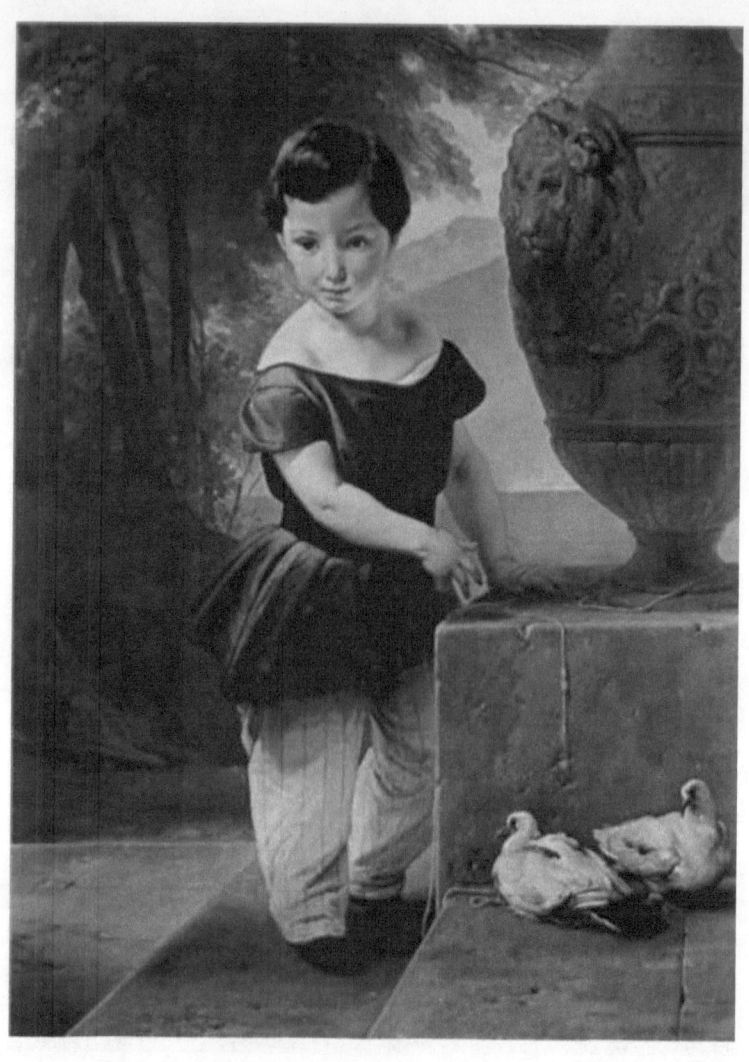

Portrait of Don Giulio Vigoni as a child, 1830, Oil on canvas

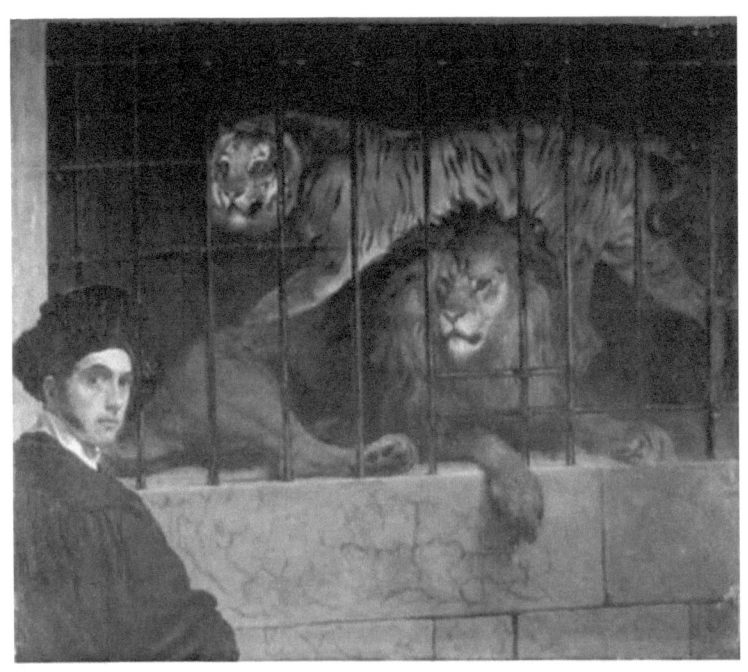

Self-portrait with Tiger and Lion1830, Oil on canvas

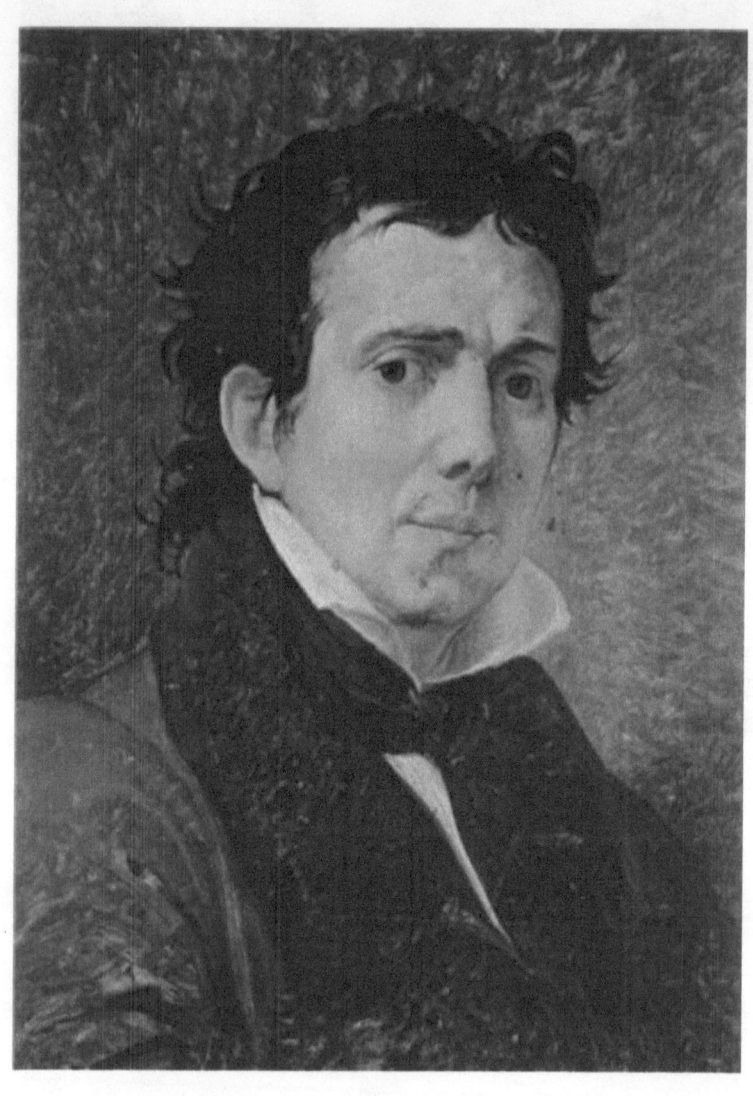

Portrait of Pompeo Marchesi, 1830, Oil on canvas

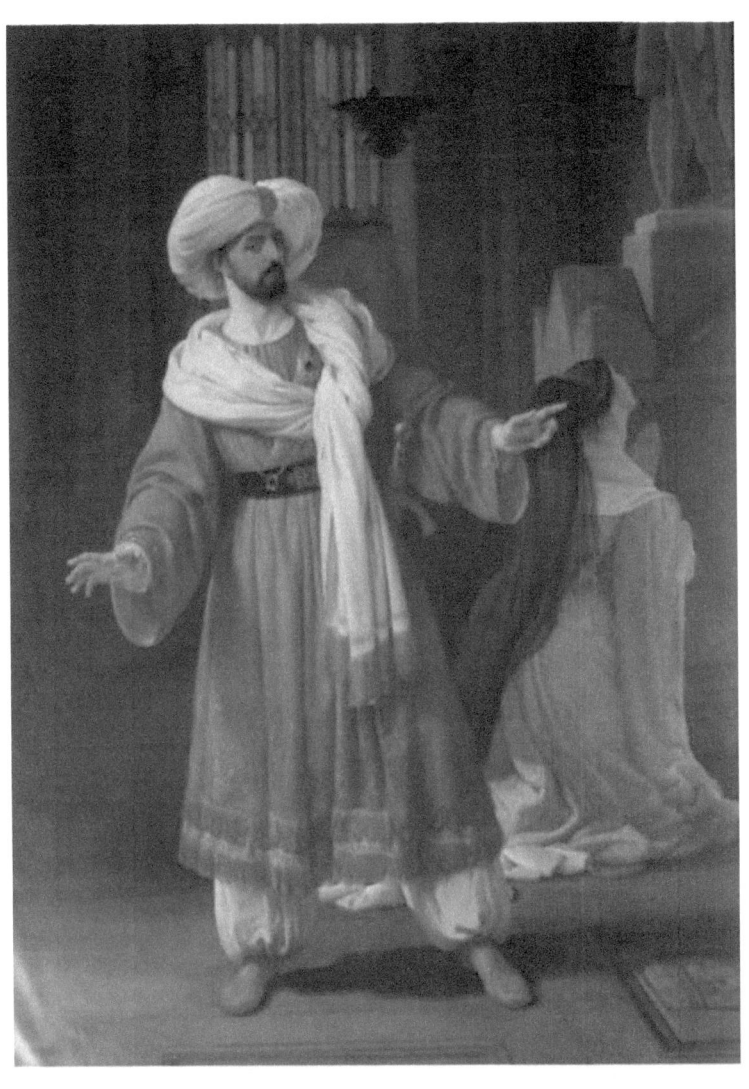

Portrait of Giovanni David as Alessandro in Pacini's Gli
arabi nelle Gallie, 1830, Oil on canvas

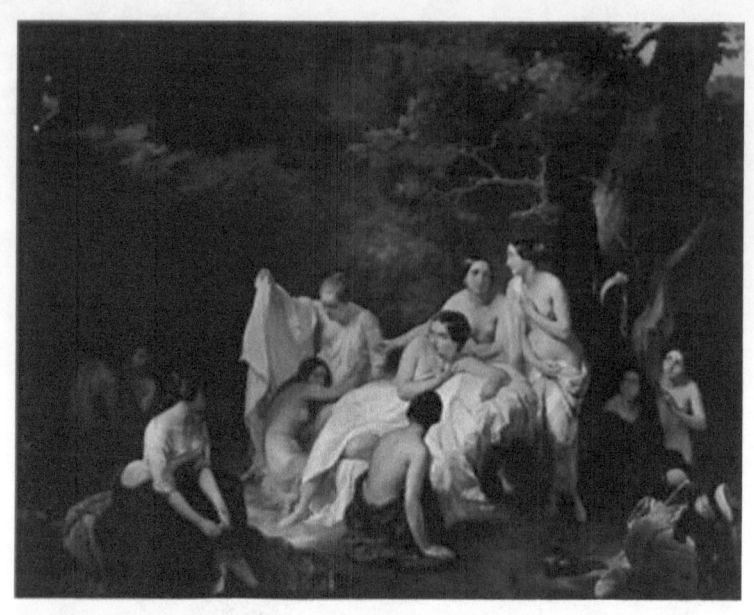

Bathing nymphs, 1831, Oil on canvas

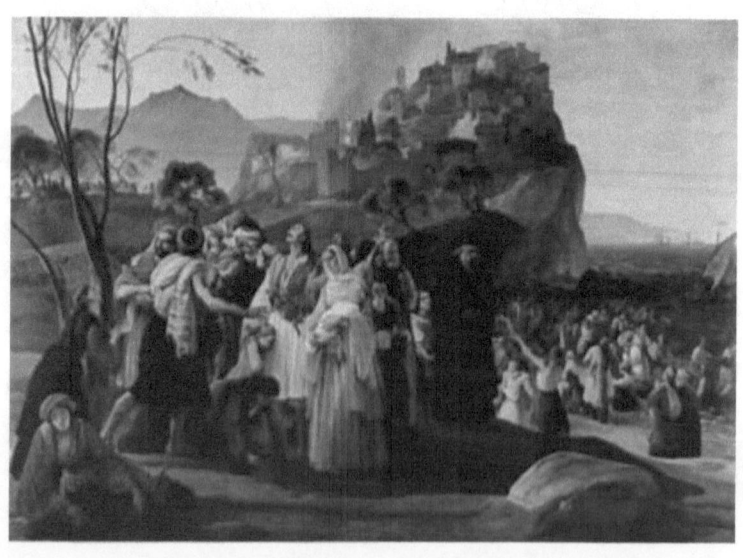

The Refugees of Parga, 1831, Oil on canvas

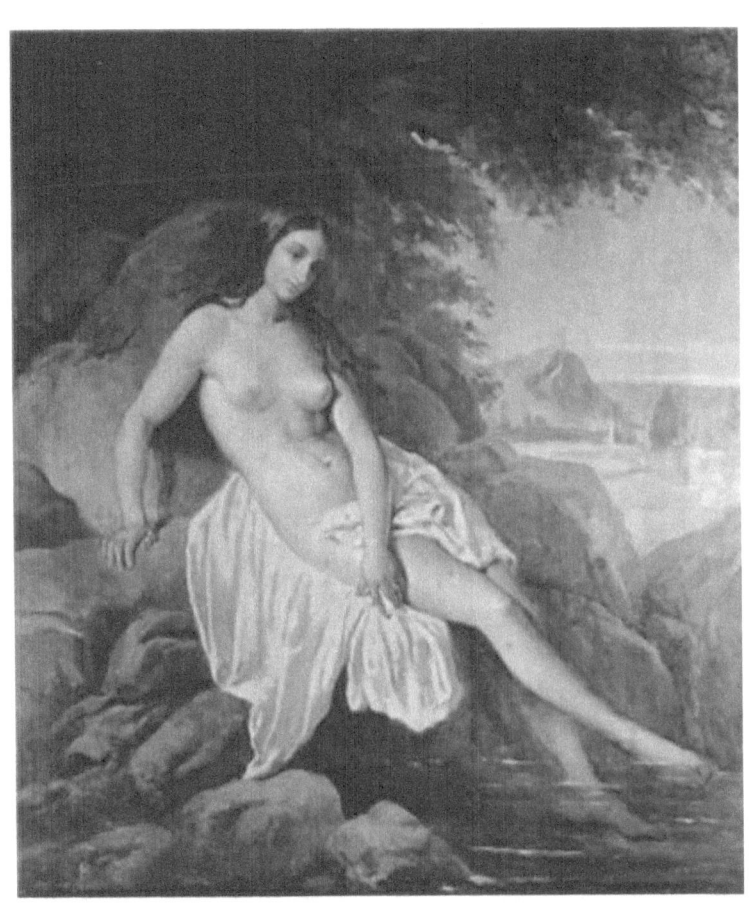

Badende, 1832, Oil on canvas

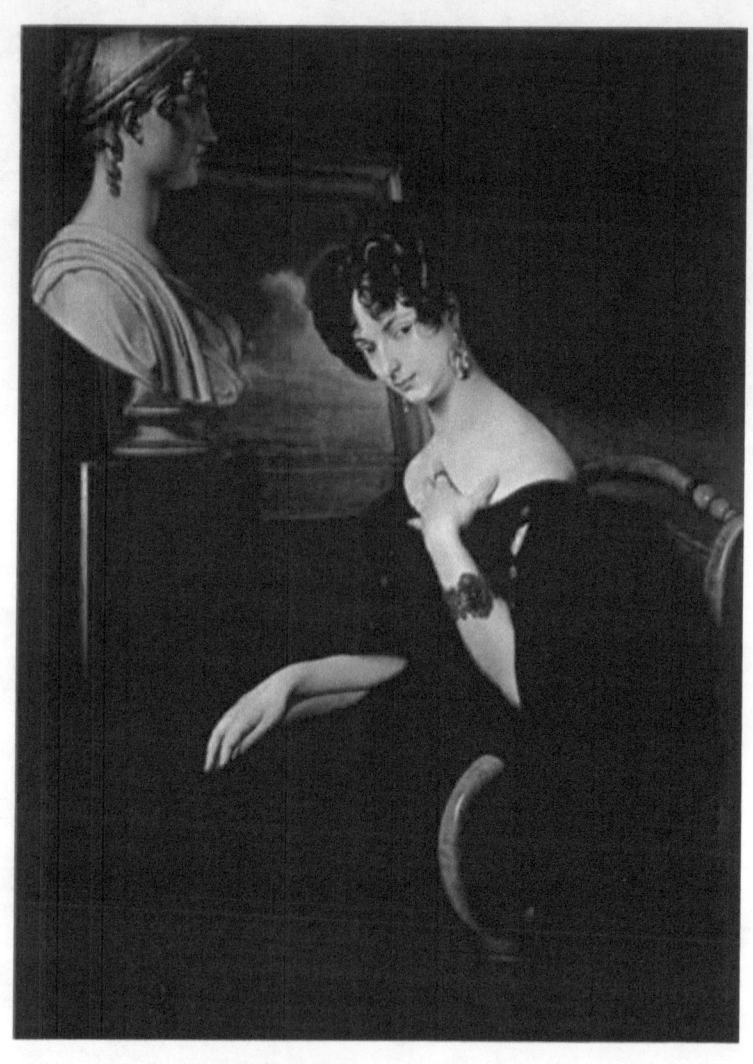

Portrait of Cristina di Belgiojoso Trivulzio, 1832, Oil on canvas

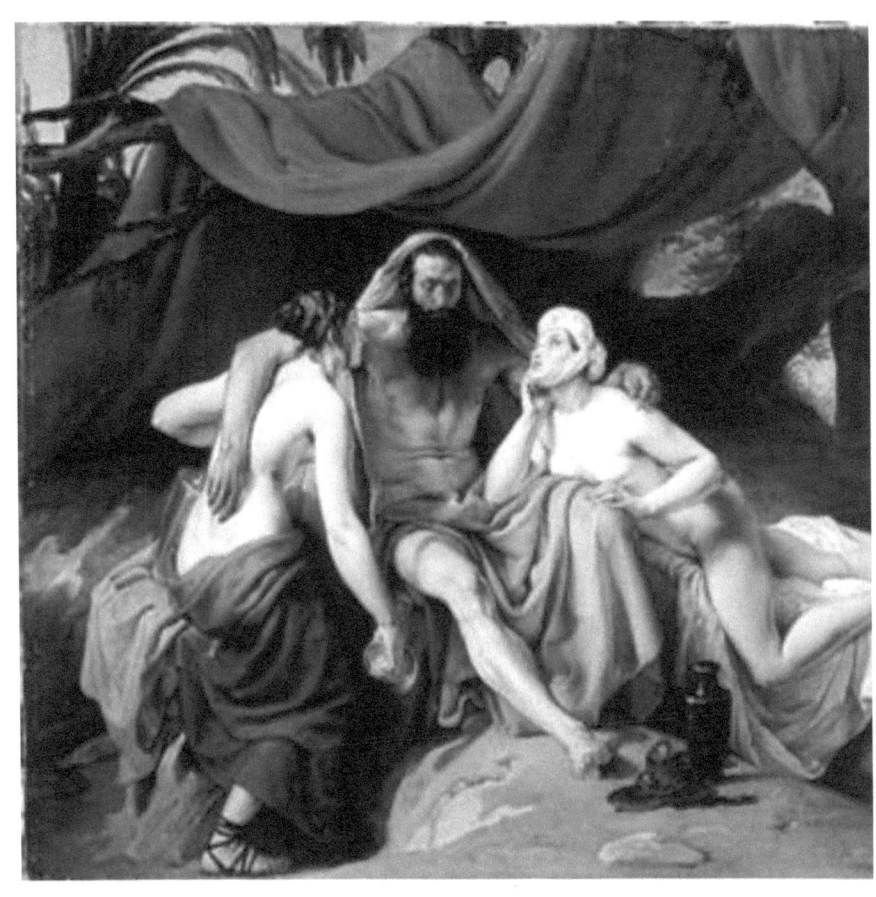

Lot and His Daughters, 1833, Oil on canvas

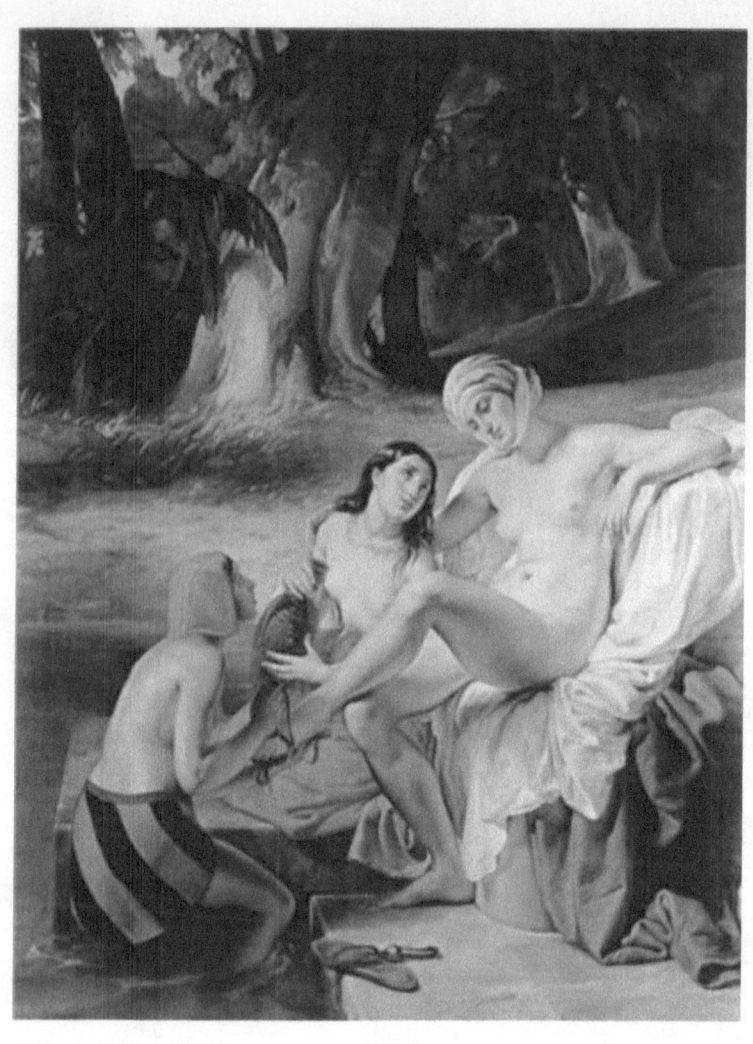

Bathing Bathsheba, 1834, Oil on canvas

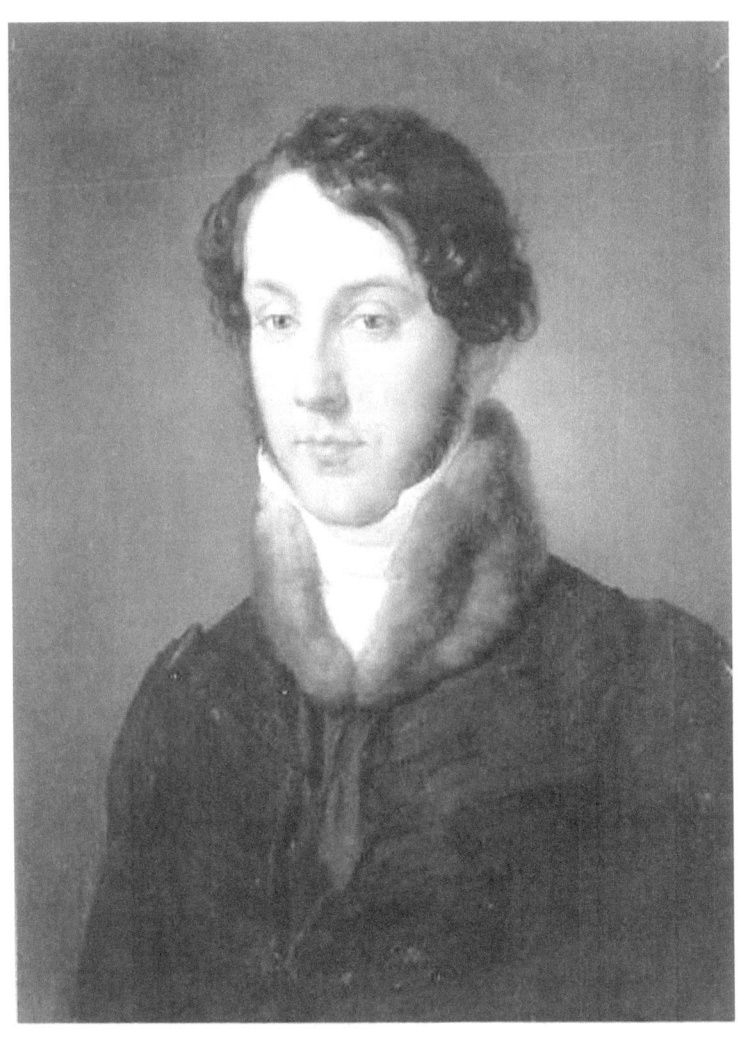

Portrait of a man (misidentified as Frédéric Chopin),
1834, Oil on canvas

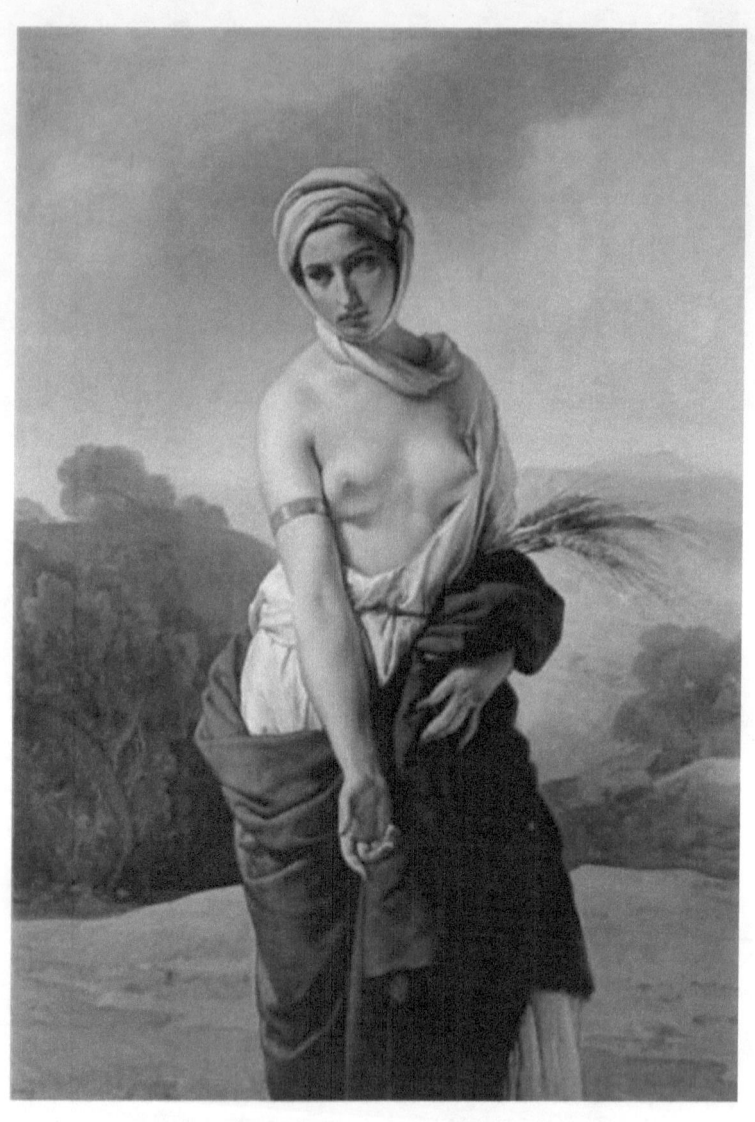

Ruth, 1835, Oil on canvas

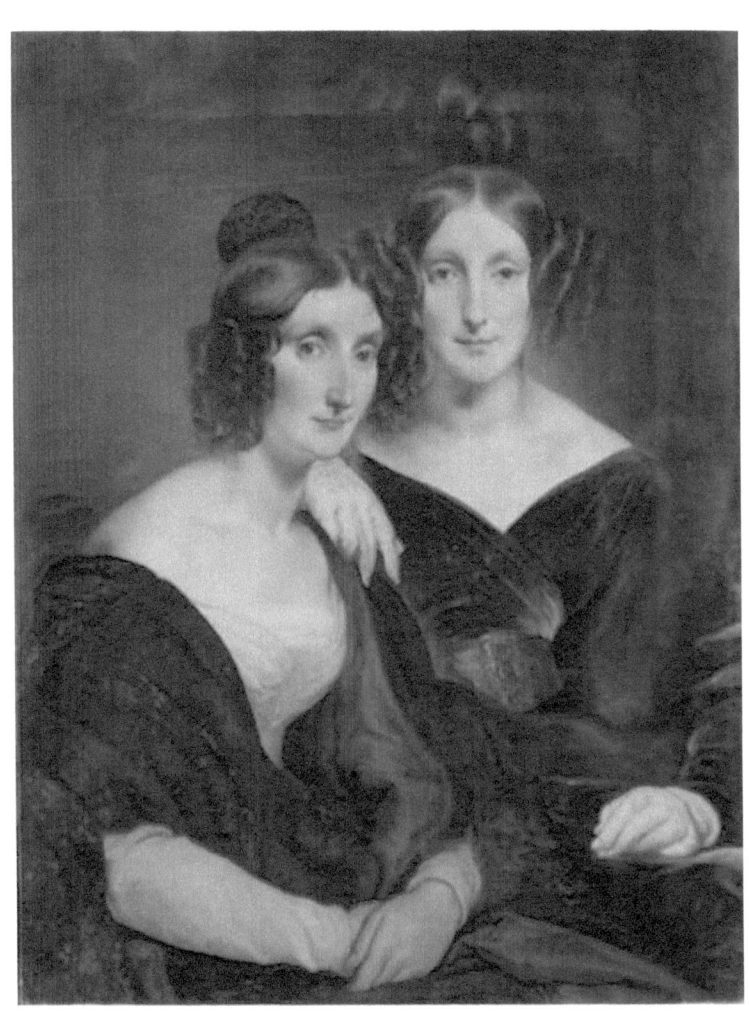

Portrait of sisters Gabrini, 1835, Oil on canvas

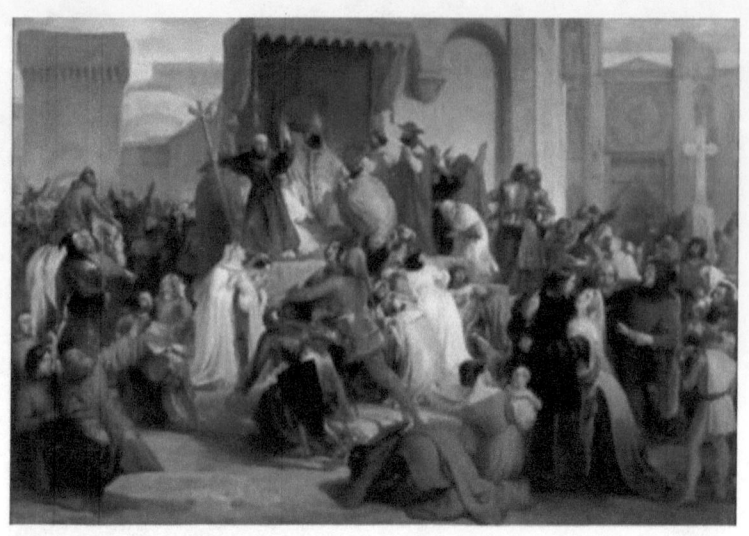

Pope Urban II Preaching the First Crusade in the
Square of Clermont, 1835, Oil on canvas

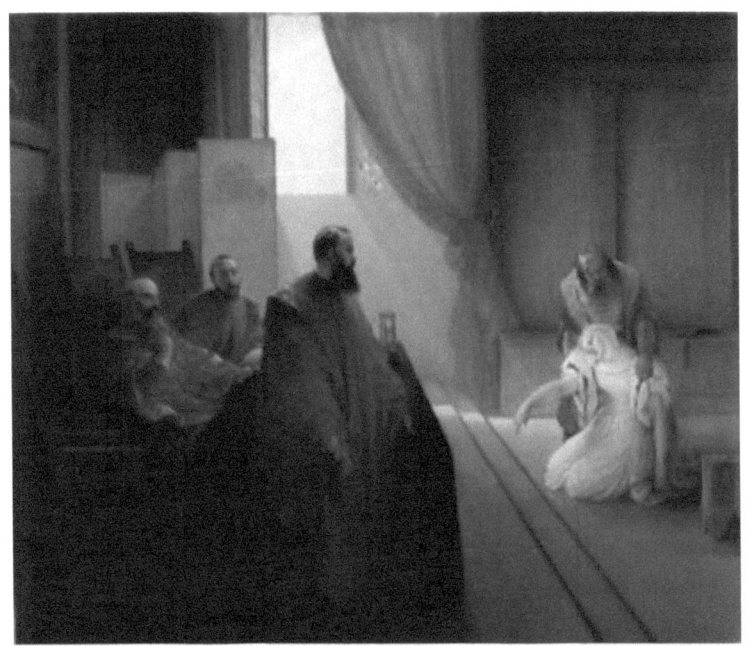

Valenza Gradenigo before the Inquisition, 1835, Oil on canvas

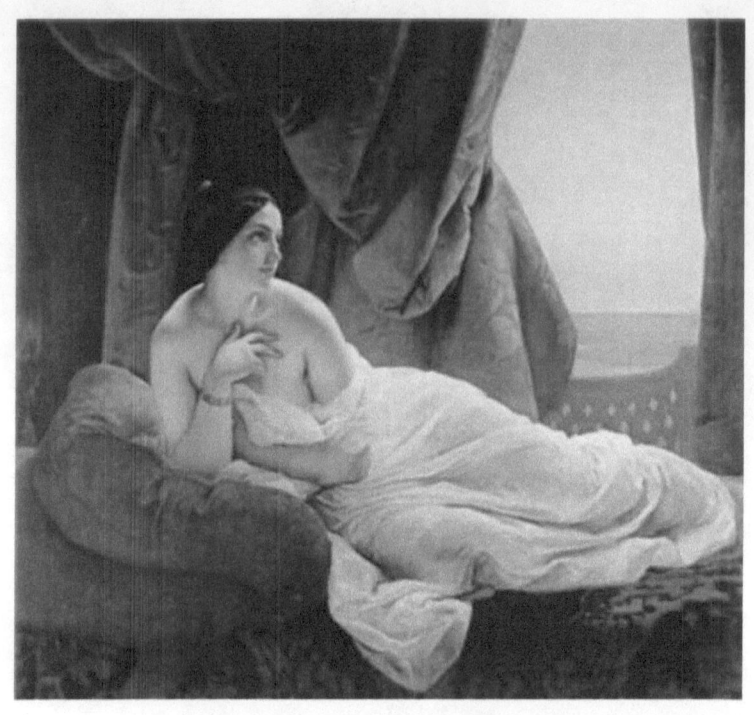

Reclining odalisque, 1839, Oil on canvas

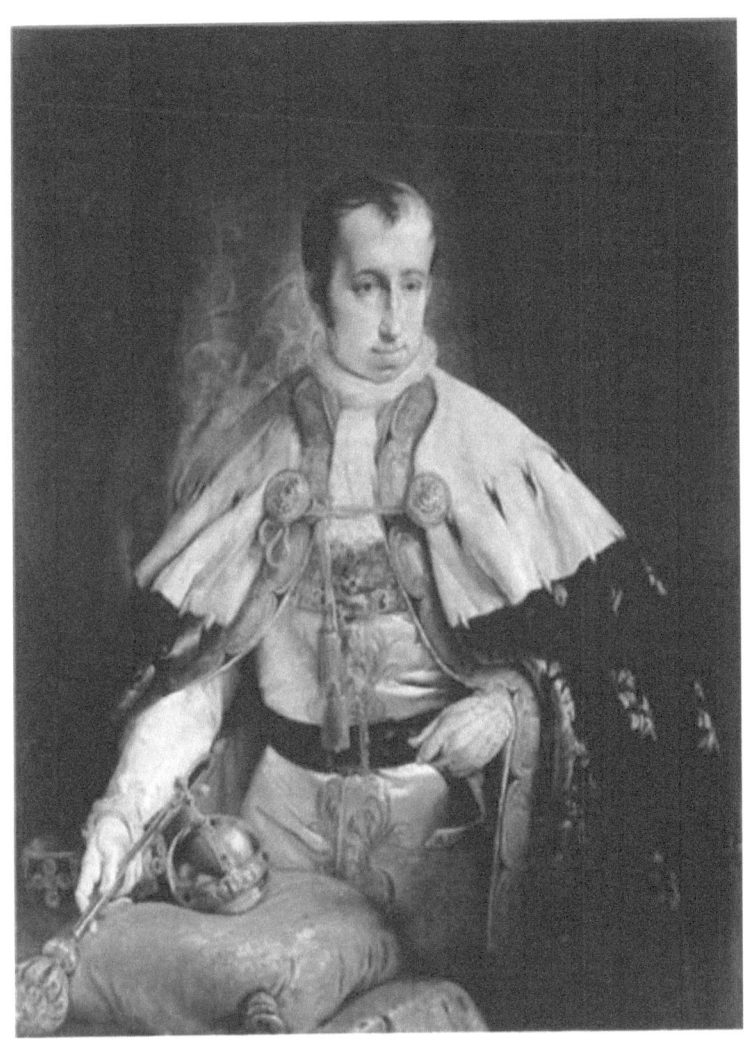

Portrait of Ferdinand I of Austria, 1840, Oil on canvas

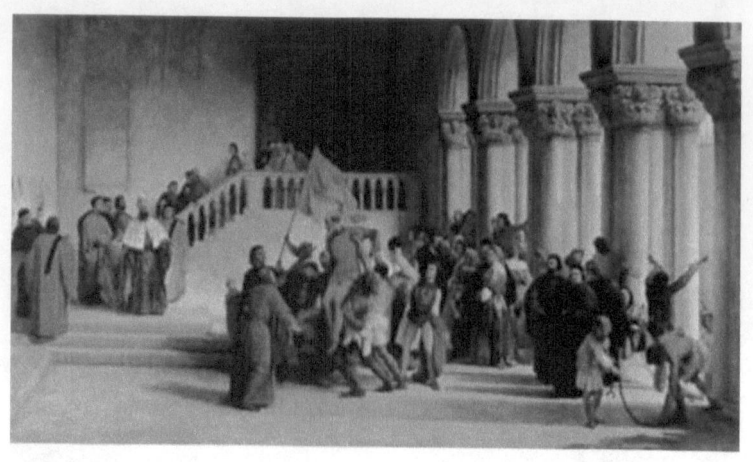

The liberation from the prison of Vettor Pisani, 1840,
Oil on canvas

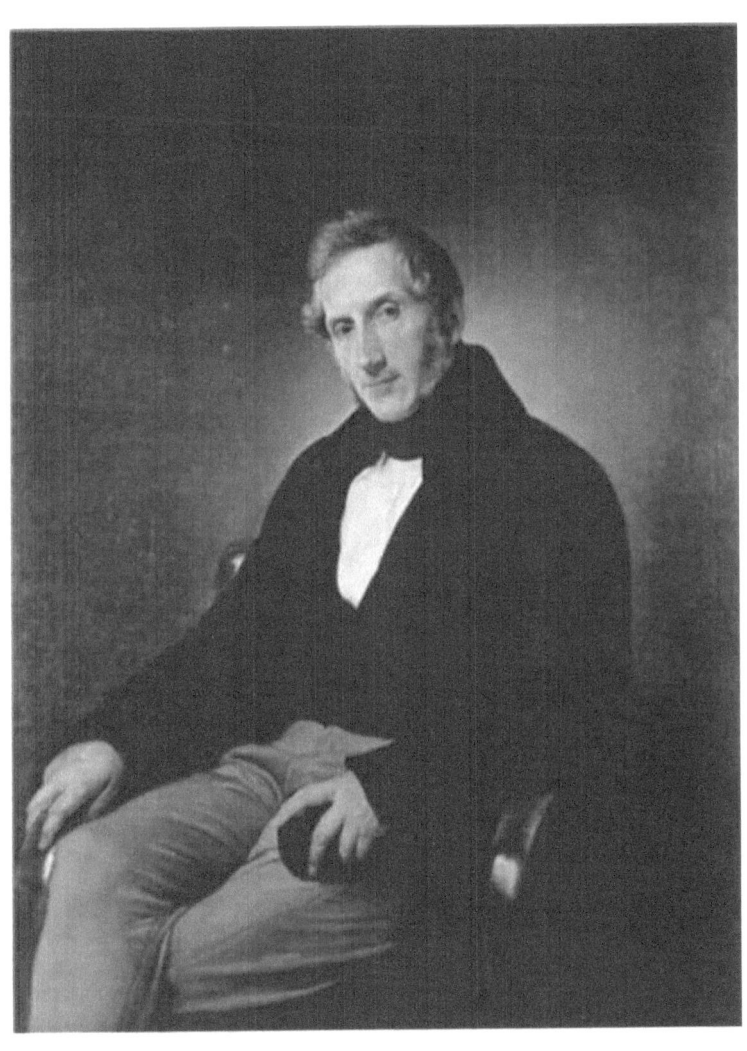

Portrait of Alessandro Manzoni, 1841, Oil on canvas

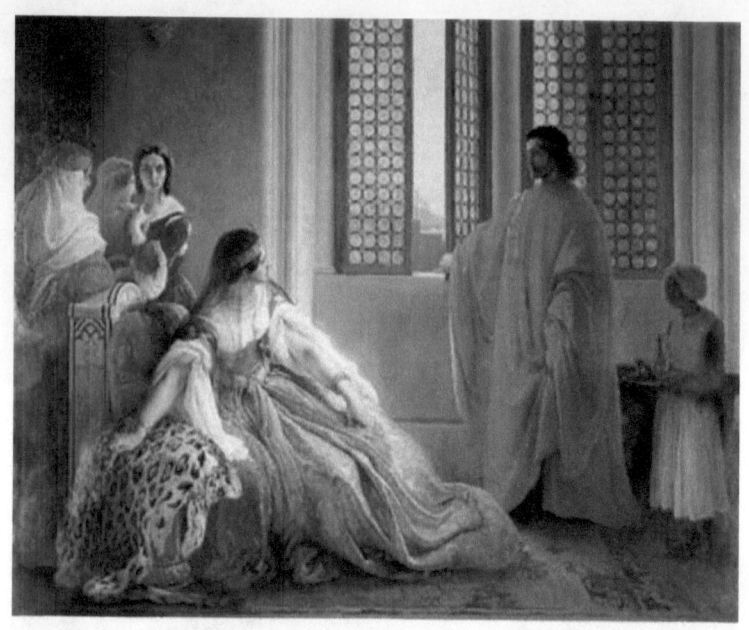

Caterina Cornaro Deposed from the Throne of Cyprus, 1842, Oil on canvas

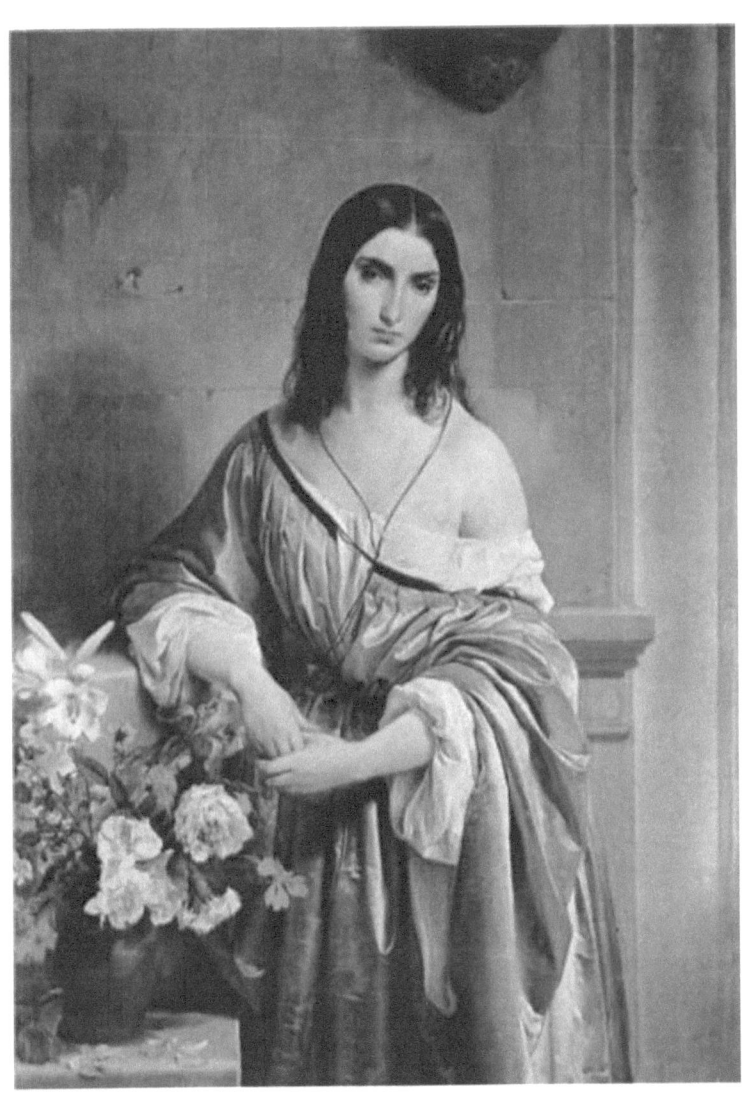

Melancholic Thoughts, 1842, Oil on canvas

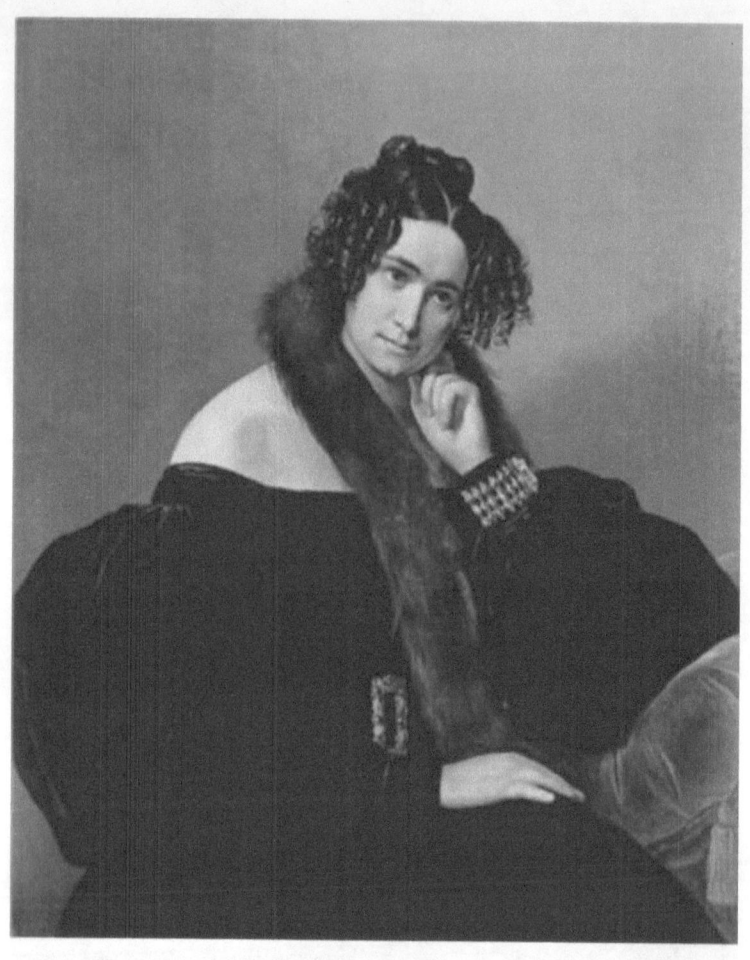

Portrait of Felicina Caglio Perego di Cremnago, 1842,
Oil on canvas

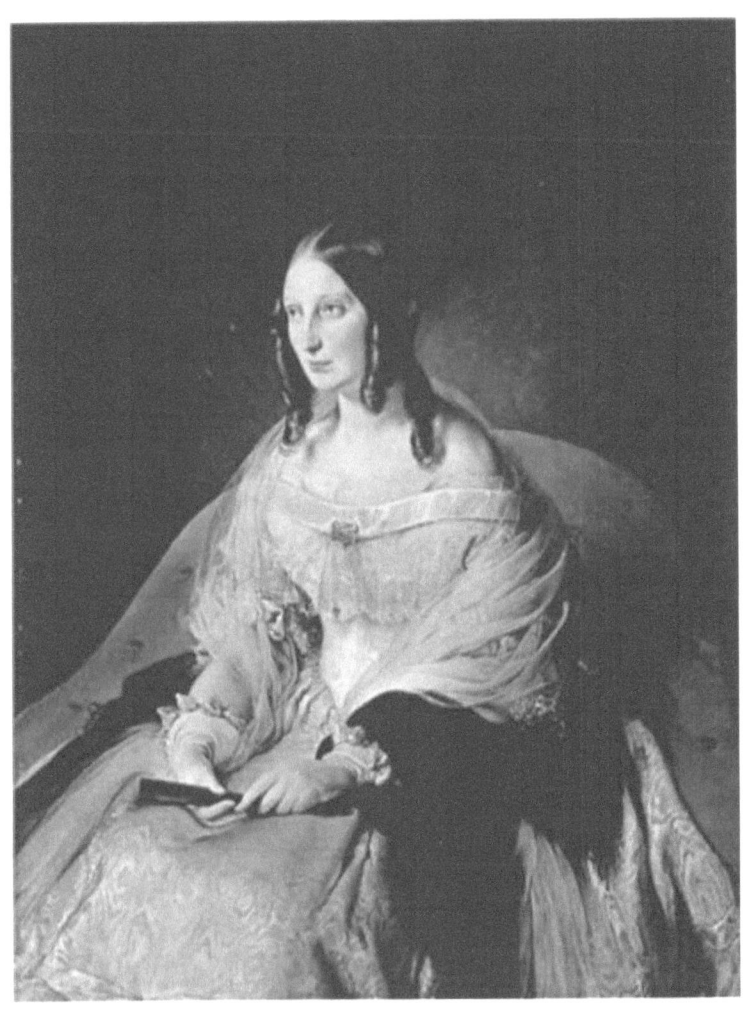

Portrait of Princess Di Sant 'Antimo, c.1842, Oil on canvas

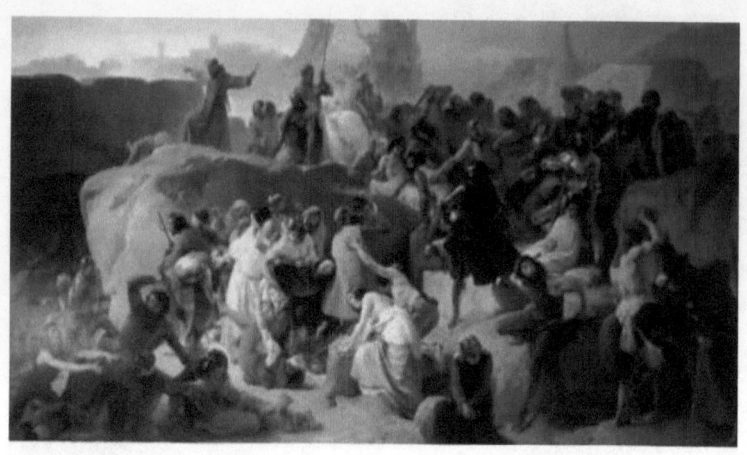

Crusaders Thirsting near Jerusalem, c.1843, Oil on canvas

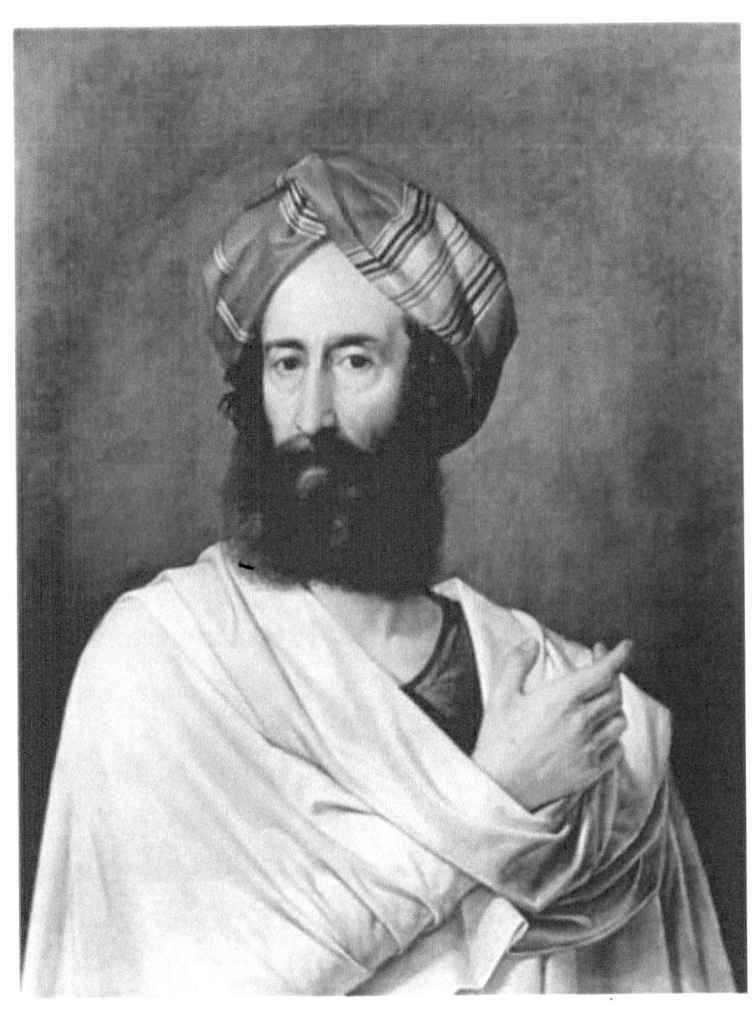

Ephraim, c.1843, Oil on canvas

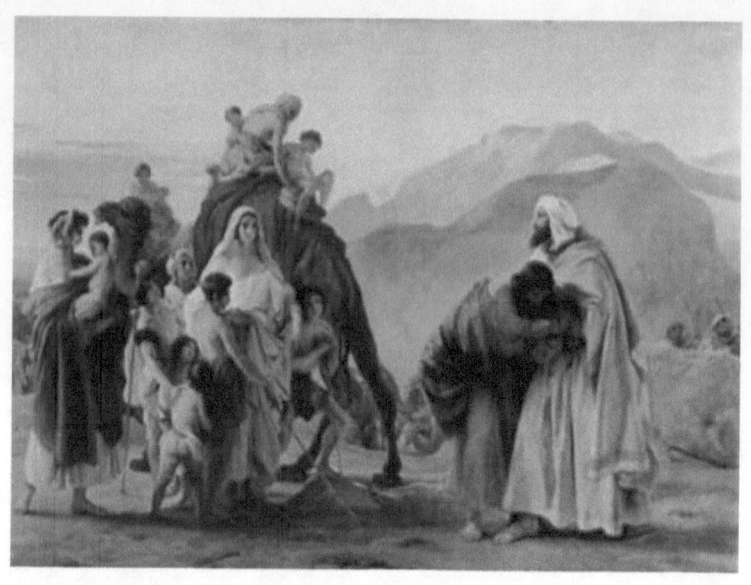

Meeting of Jacob and Esau, 1844, Oil on canvas

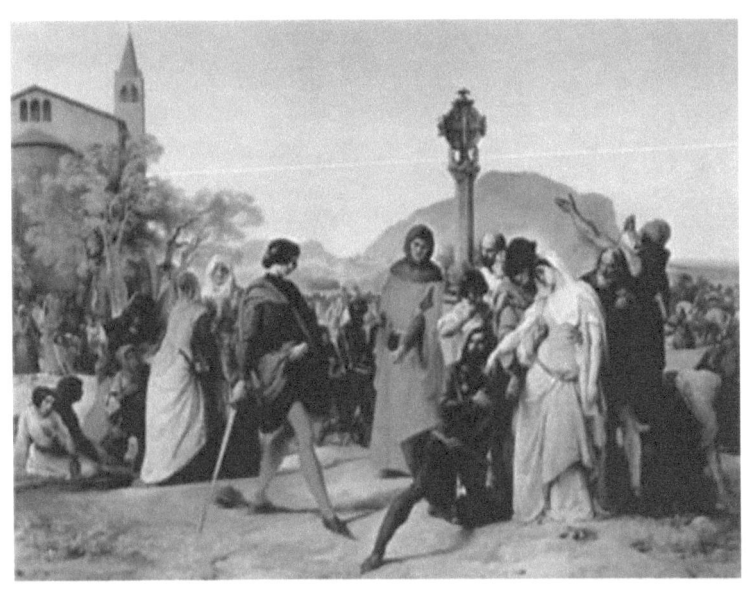

Sicilian evenings painting series, Scene 3, 1846, Oil on canvas

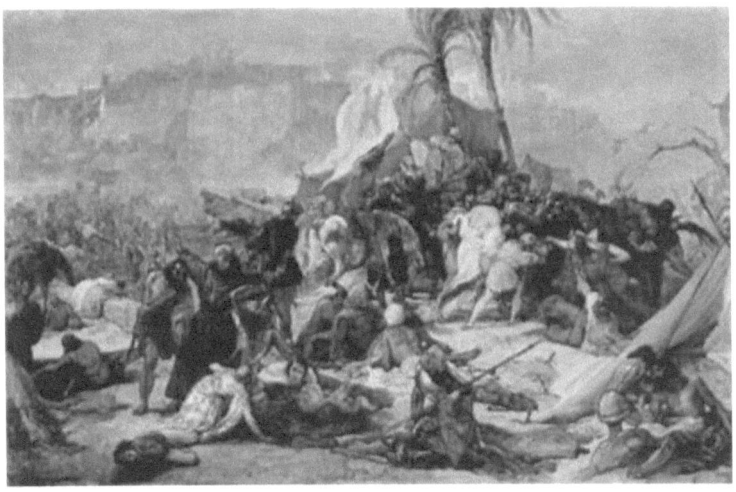

The seventh crusade against Jerusalem, c.1846, Oil on canvas

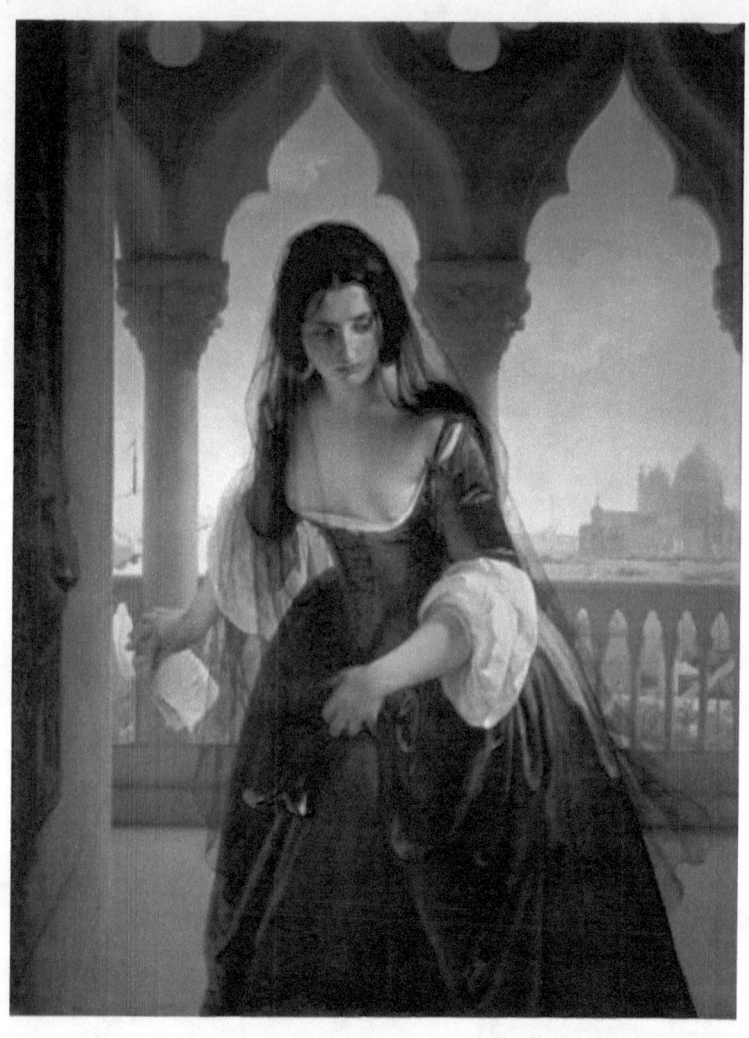

Secret indictment, 1847, Oil on canvas

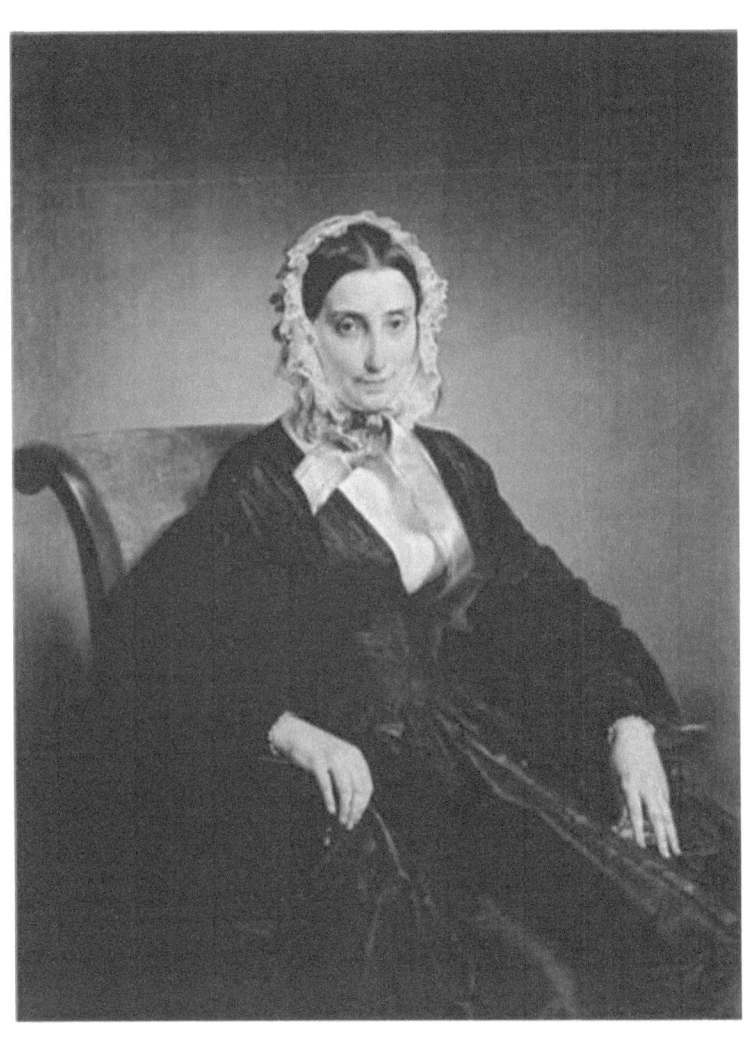

Portrait of Teresa Borri, c.1848, Oil on canvas

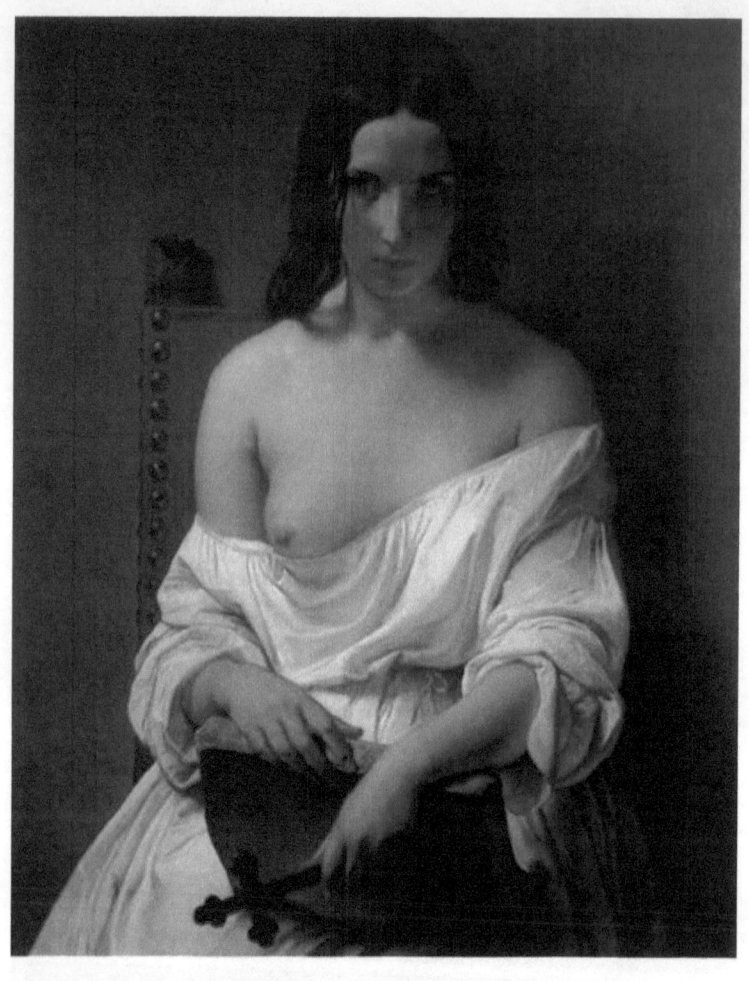

Meditation on the History of Italy, 1850, Oil on canvas

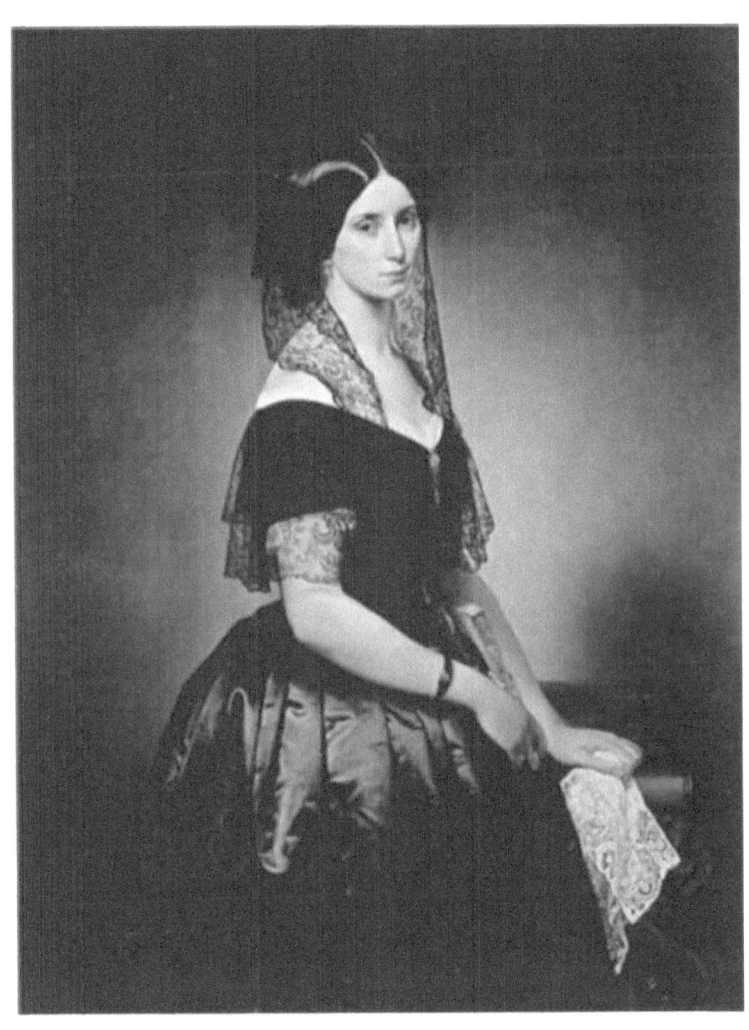

Portrait of Antoniet Tarsis Basilico, 1851, Oil on canvas

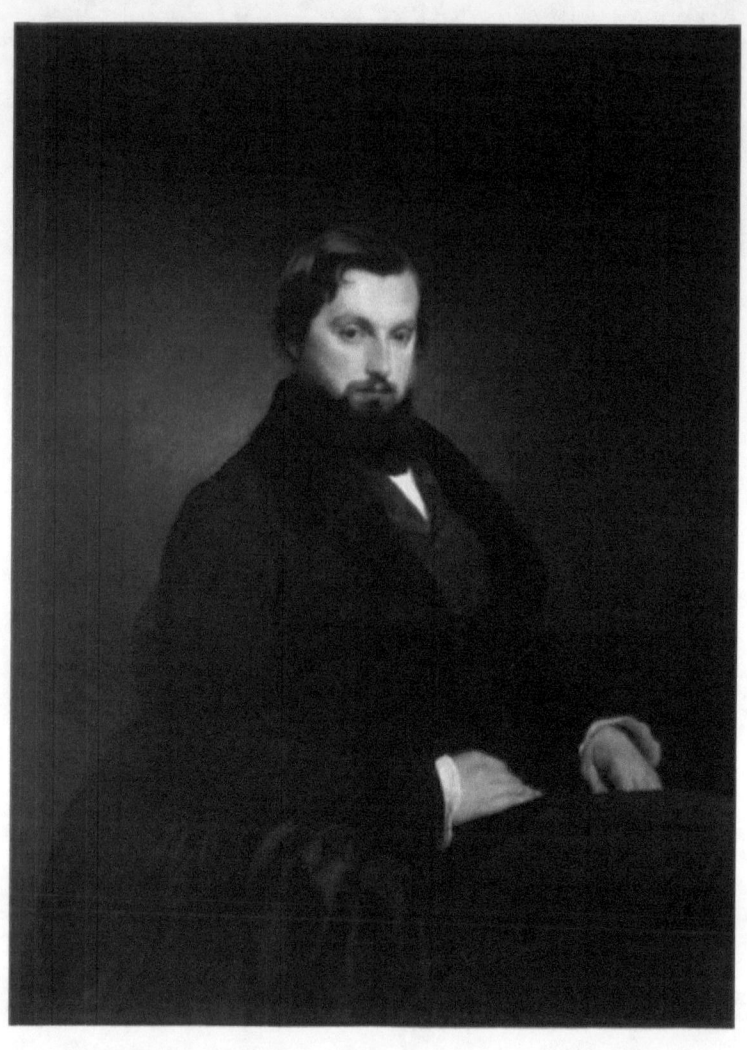

Portrait of Gian Giacomo Poldi Pezzoli, c.1851, Oil on canvas

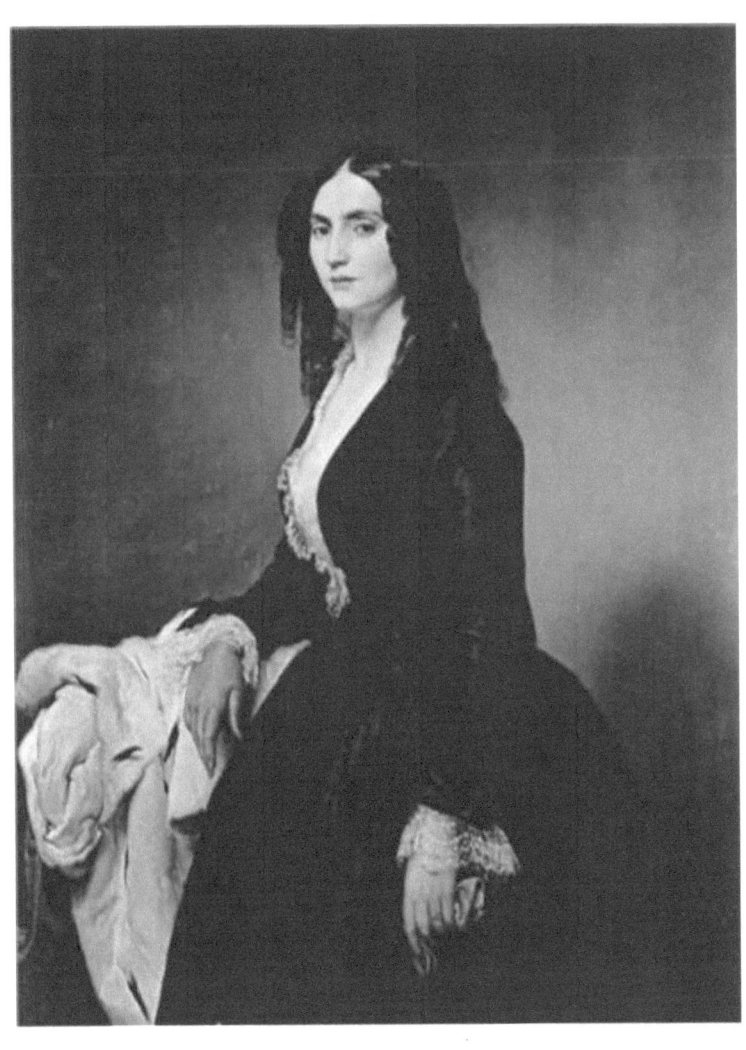

Portrait of Matilde Juva Branca, 1851, Oil on canvas

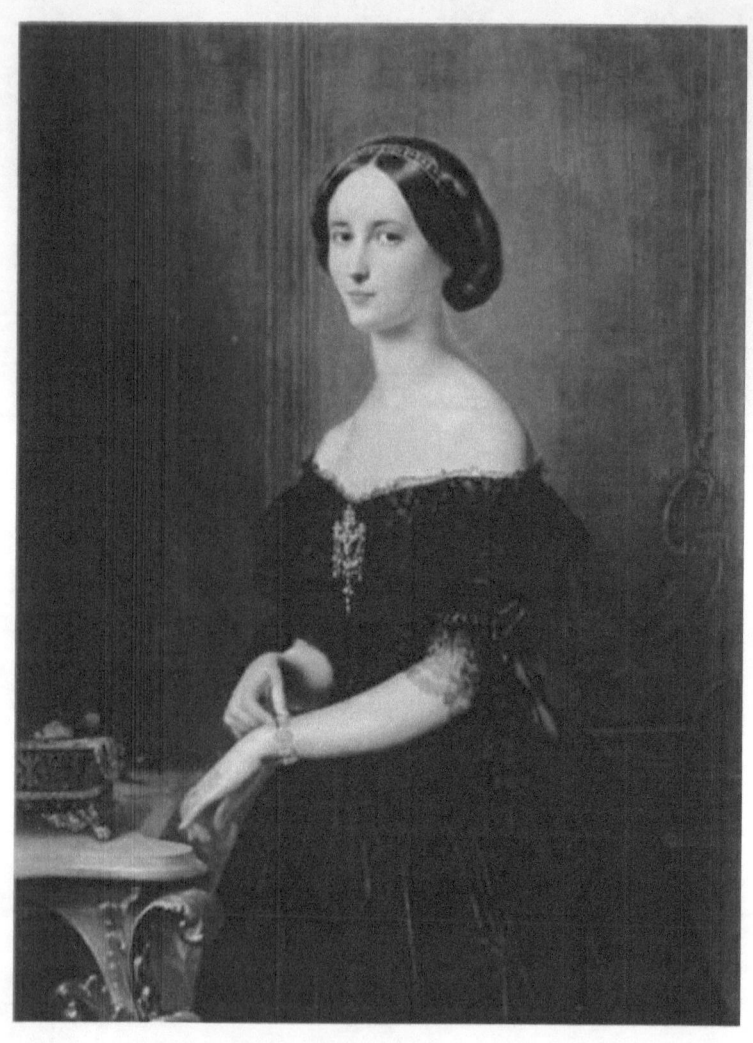

Portrait of a Venetian woman, c.1852, Oil on canvas

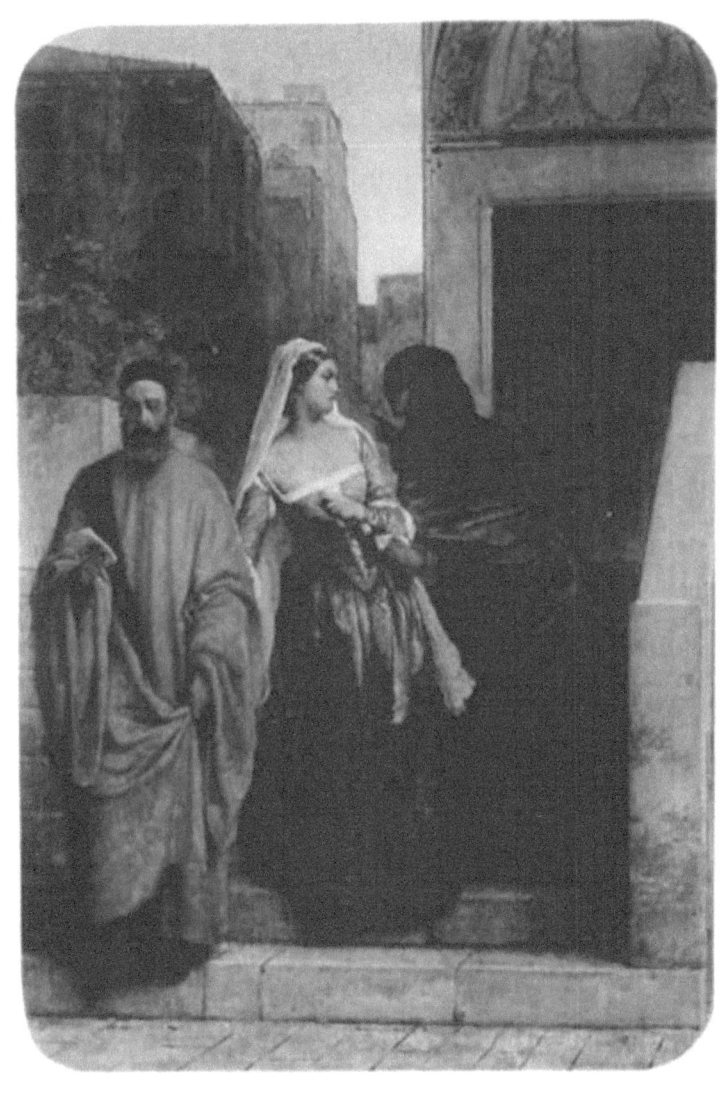

Venetian women, 1853, Oil on canvas

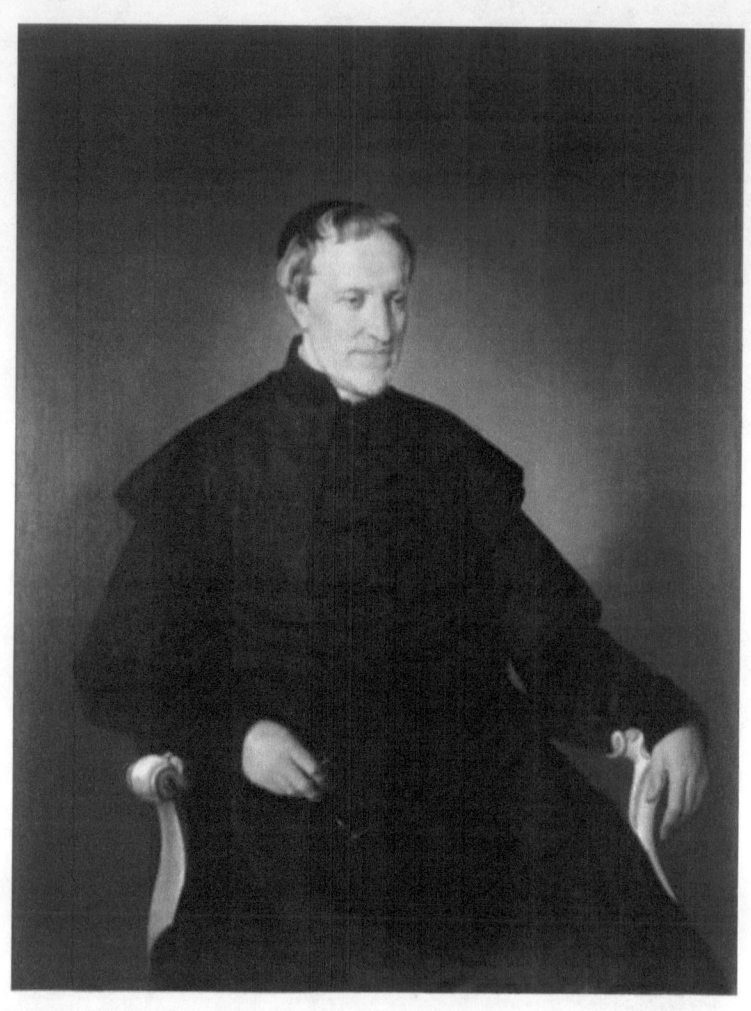

Antonio Rosmini, 1853, Oil on canvas

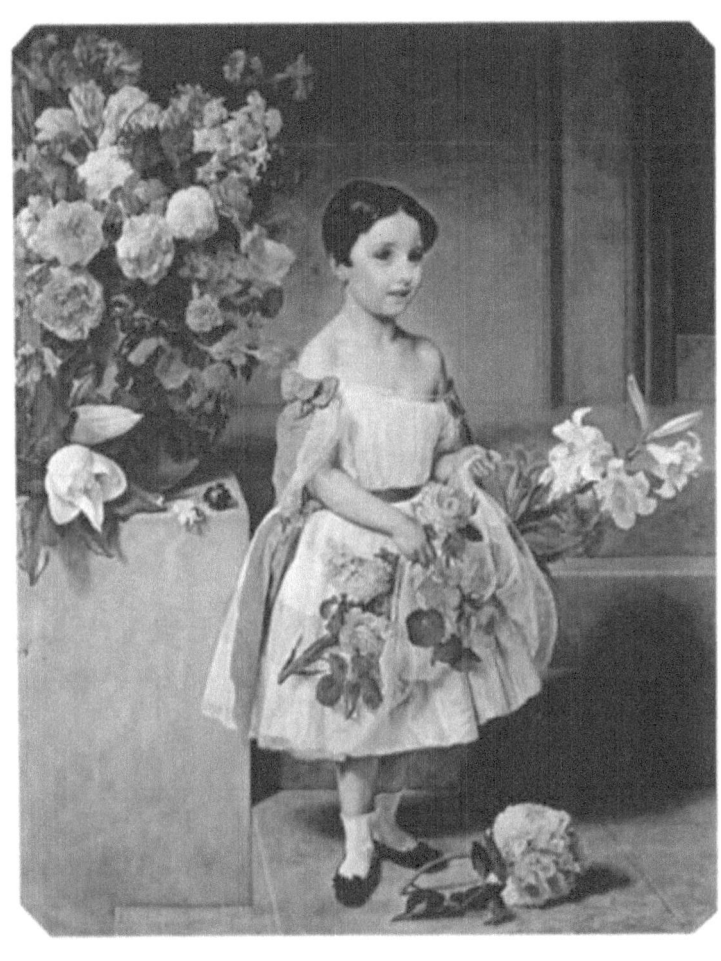

Portrait of Antoniet Negroni Prati Morosini as child,
1858, Oil on canvas

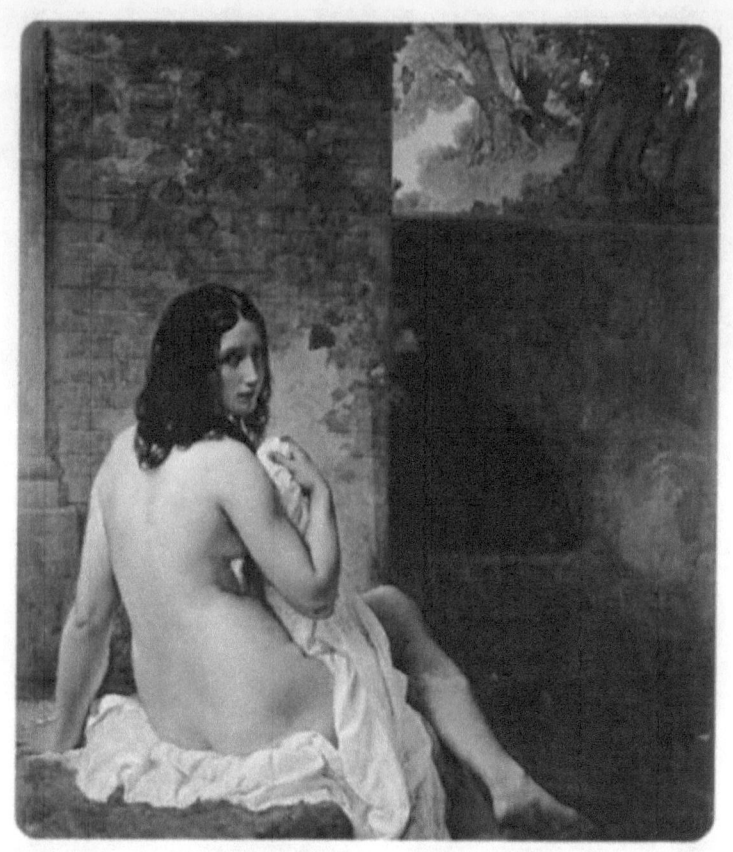

Back view of a bather, 1859, Oil on canvas

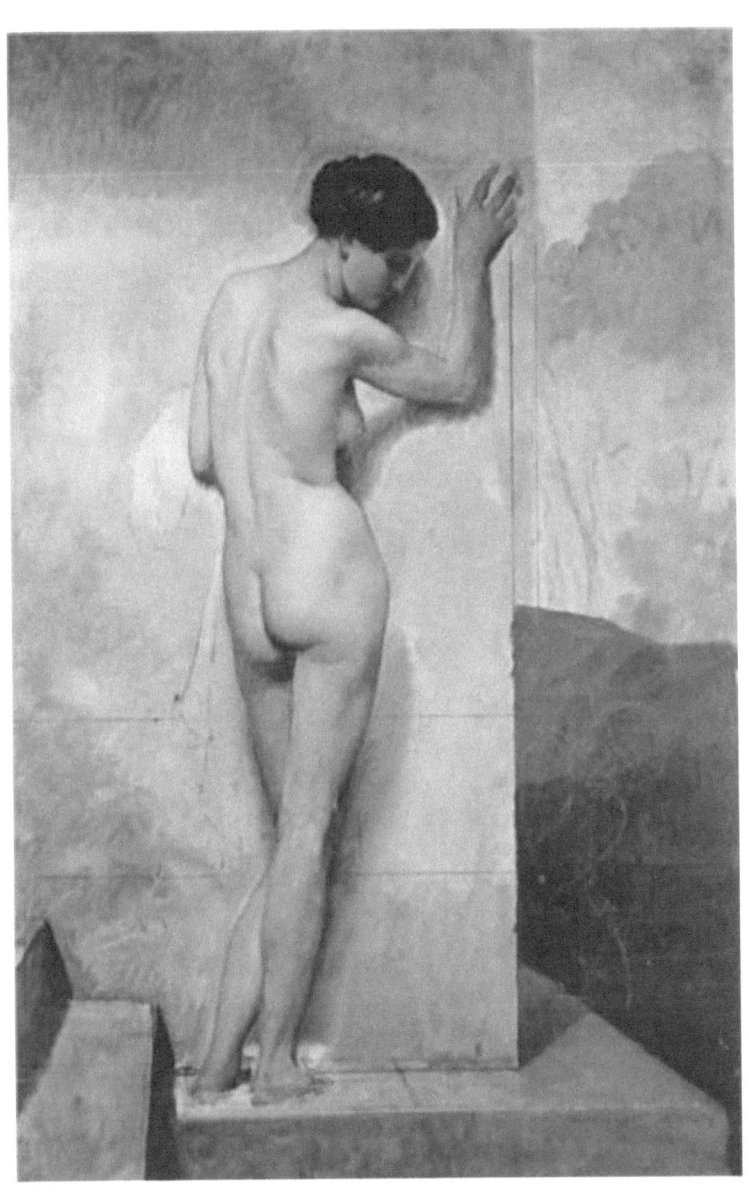

Female nude, 1859, Oil on canvas

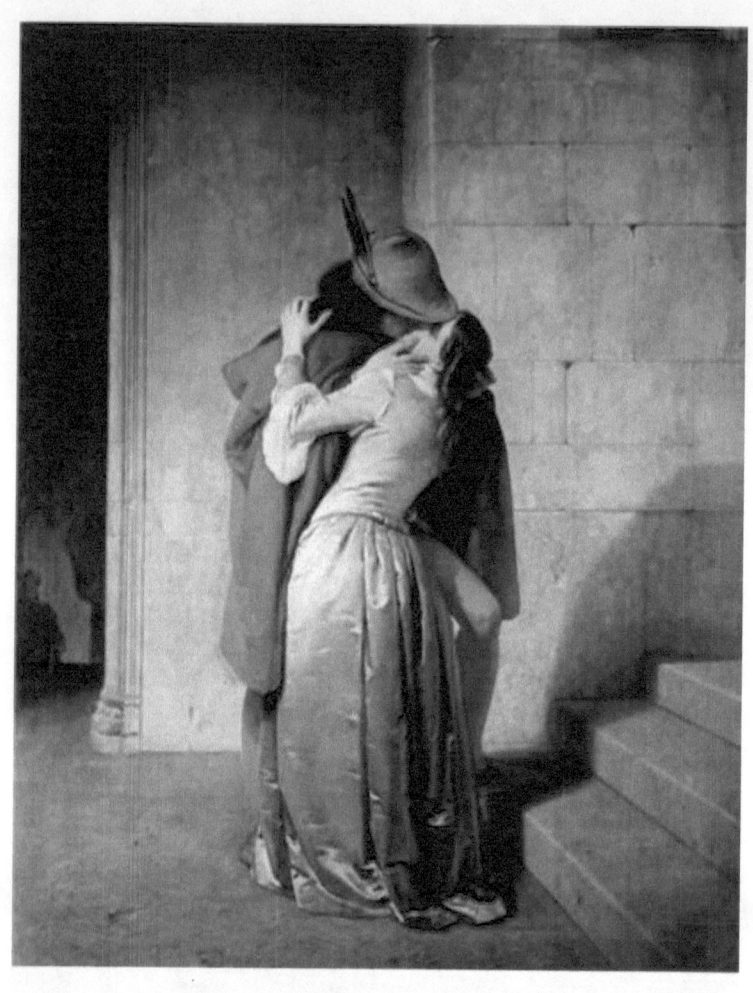

The Kiss, 1859, Oil on canvas

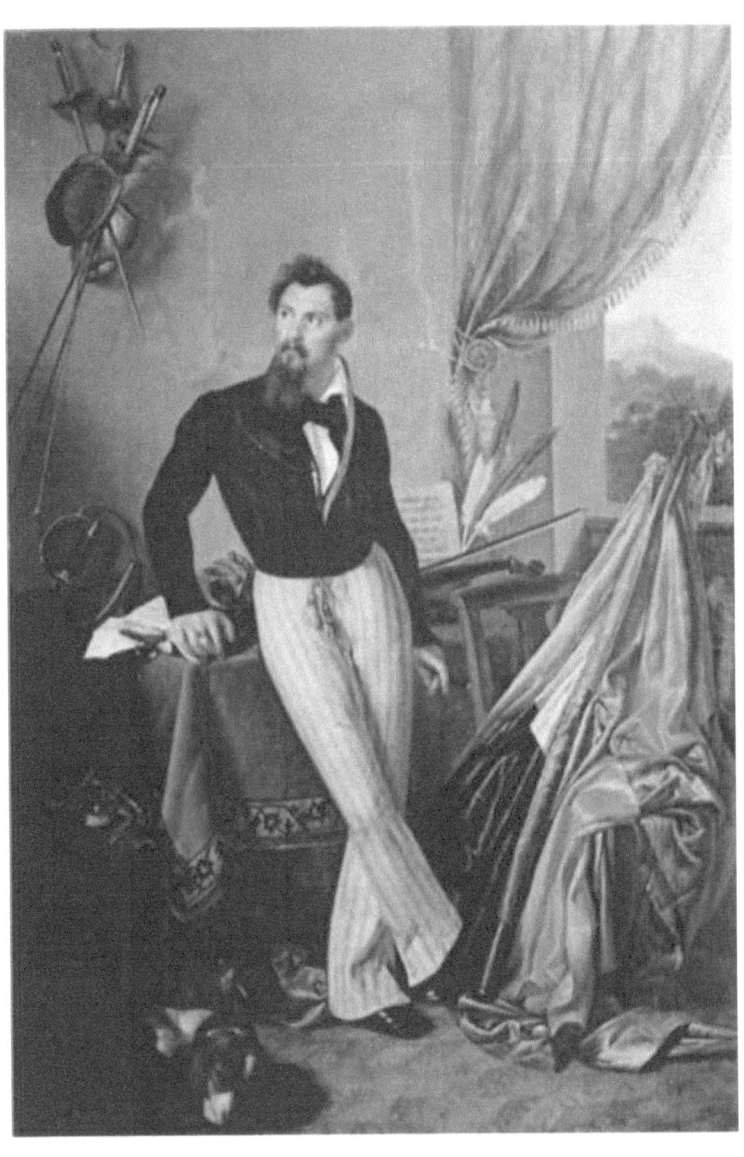

Portrait of Conte Baglioni, c.1860, Oil on canvas

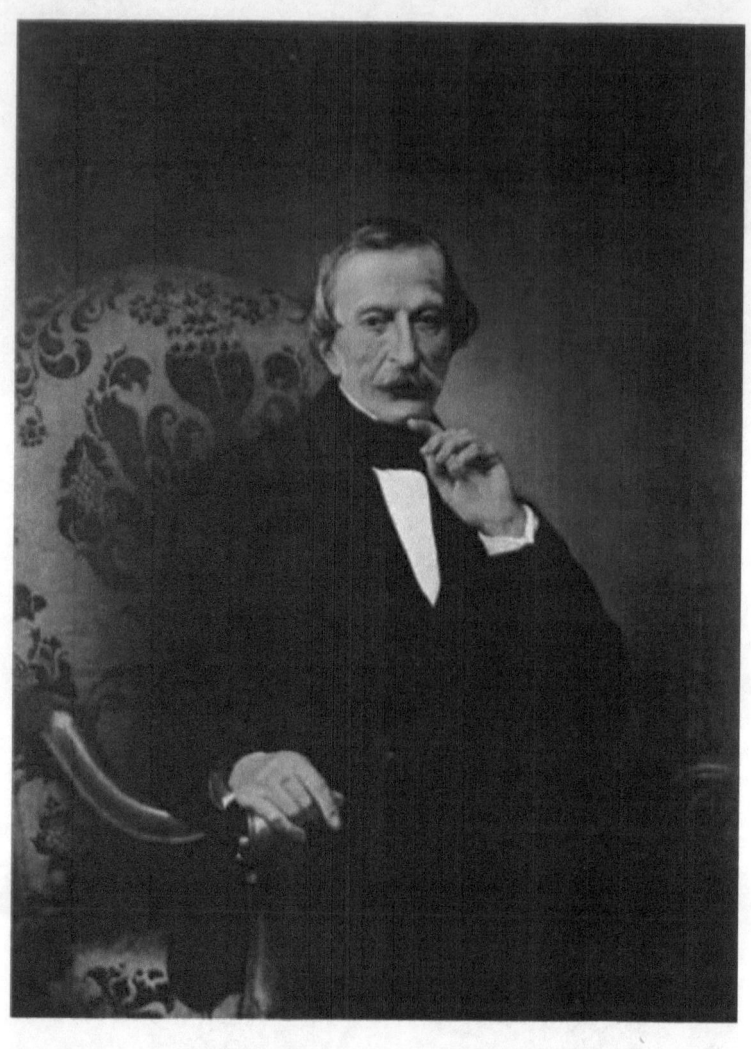

Portrait of Massimo d'Azeglio, 1860, Oil on canvas

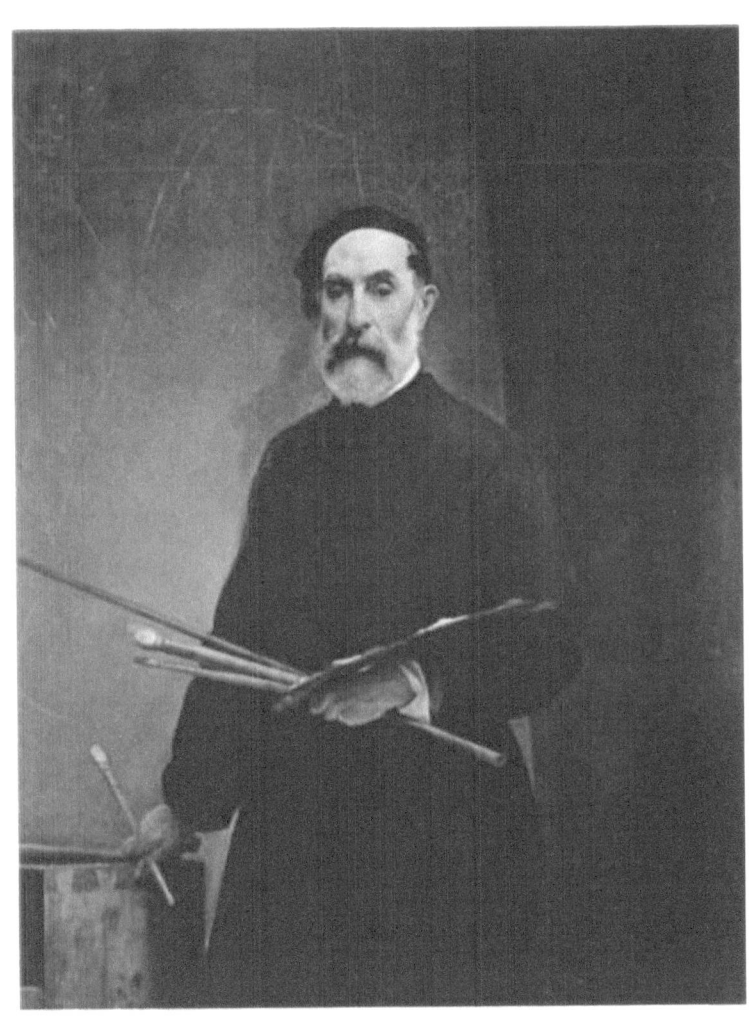

Self Portrait, c.1861, Oil on canvas

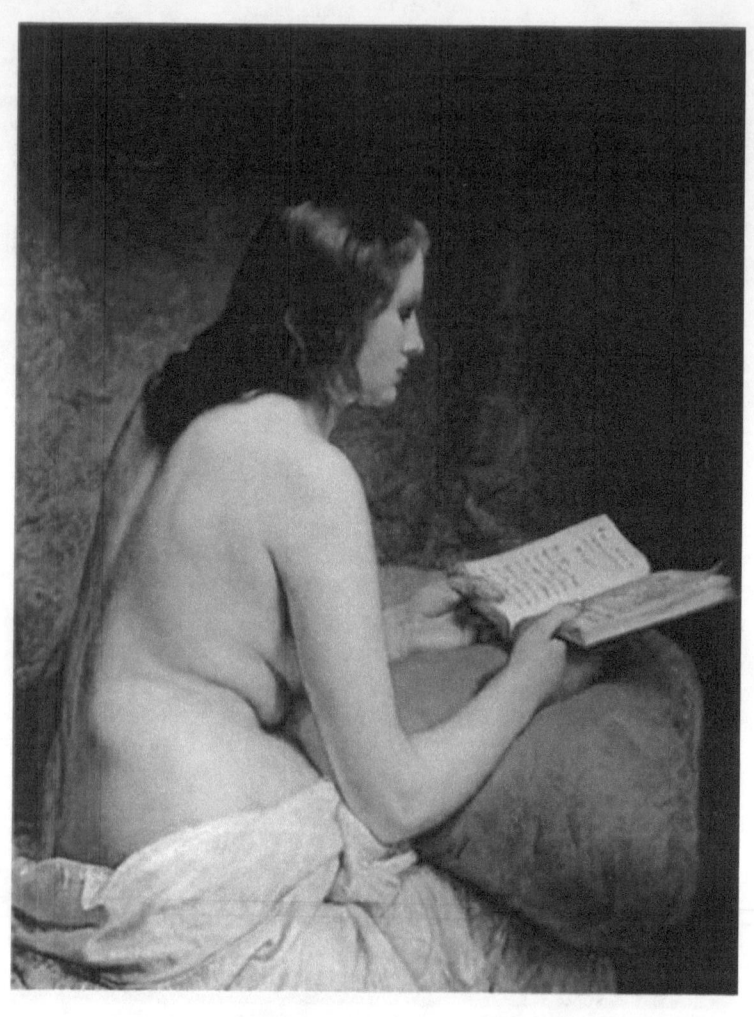

Odalisque with Book, 1866, Oil on canvas

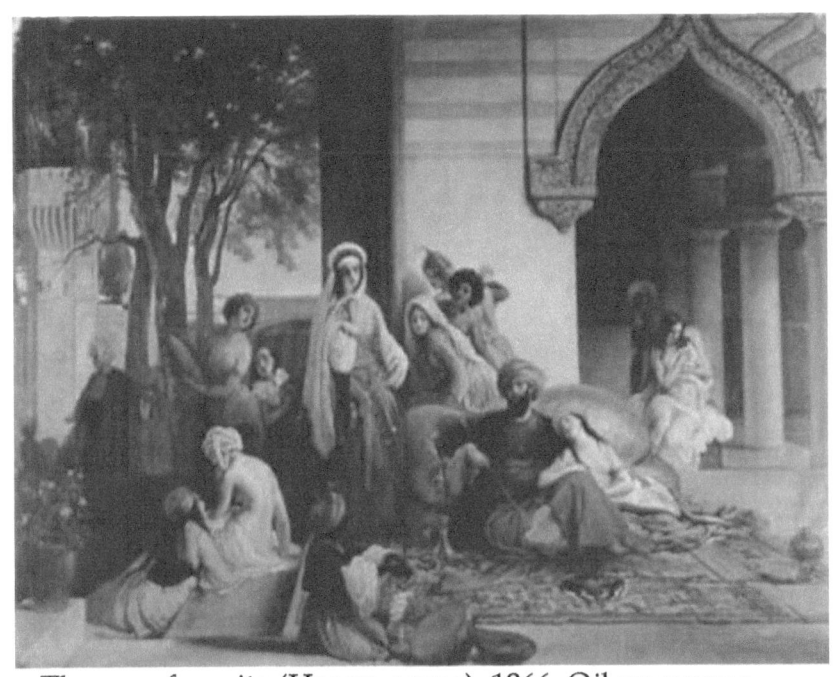

The new favorite (Harem scene), 1866, Oil on canvas

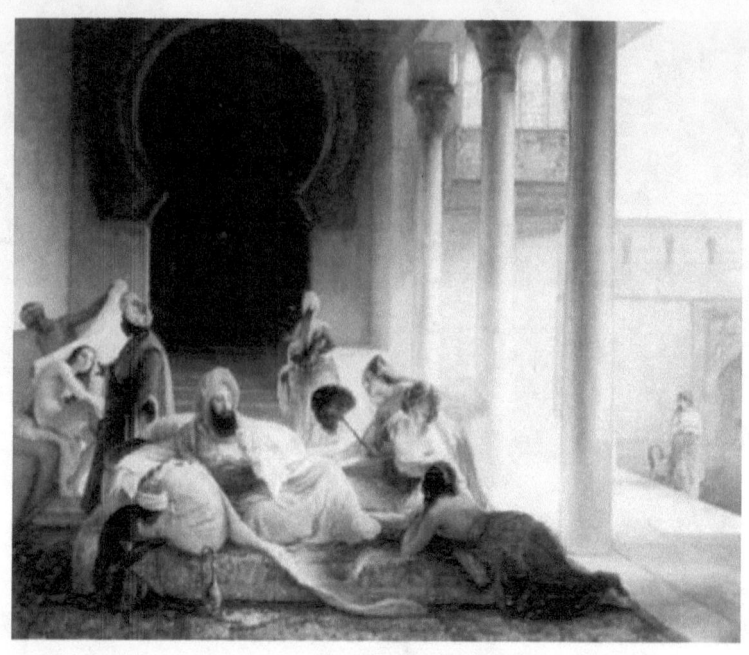

Inside the Harem, 1867, Oil on canvas

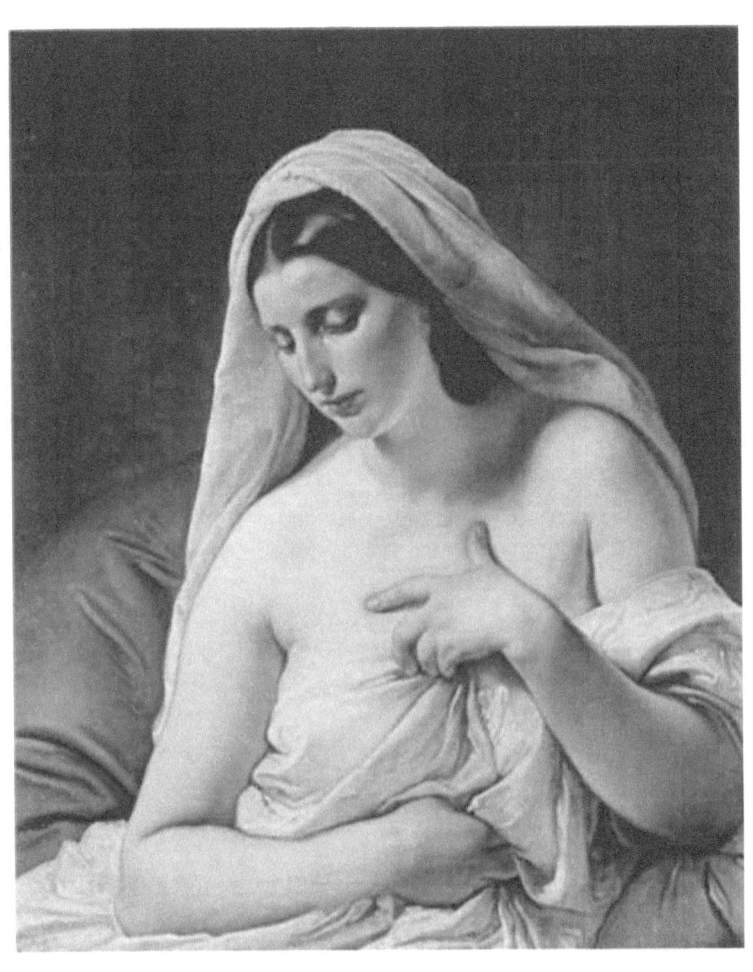

Odalisque, 1867, Oil on canvas

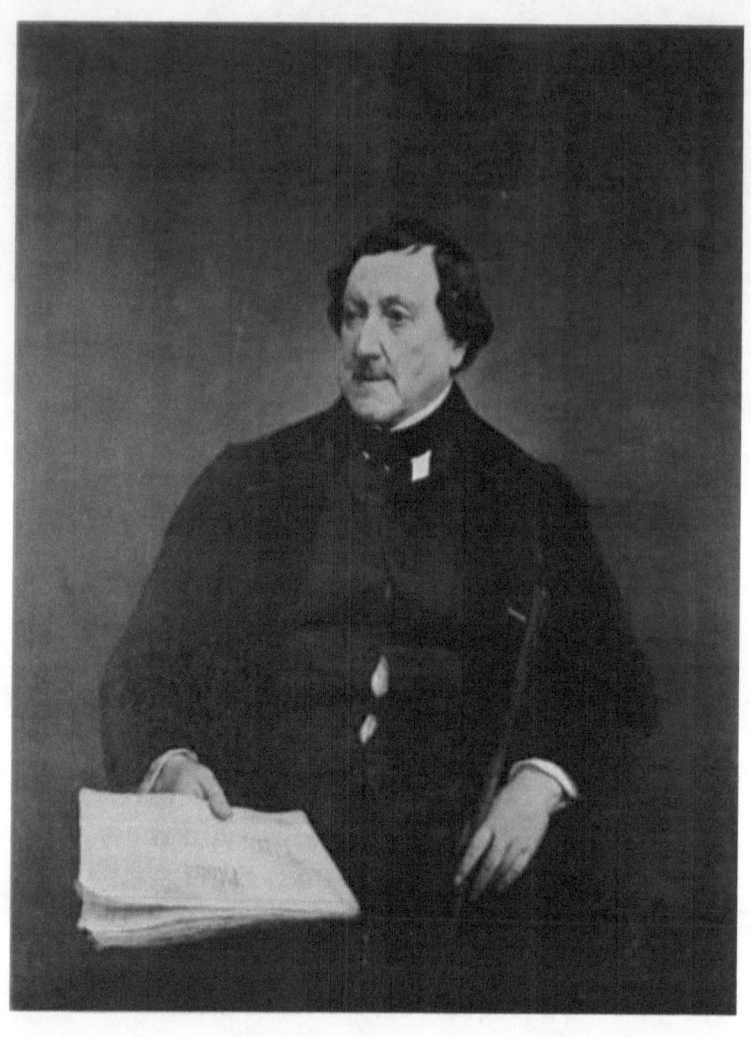

Portrait of Gioacchino Rossini, 1870, Oil on canvas

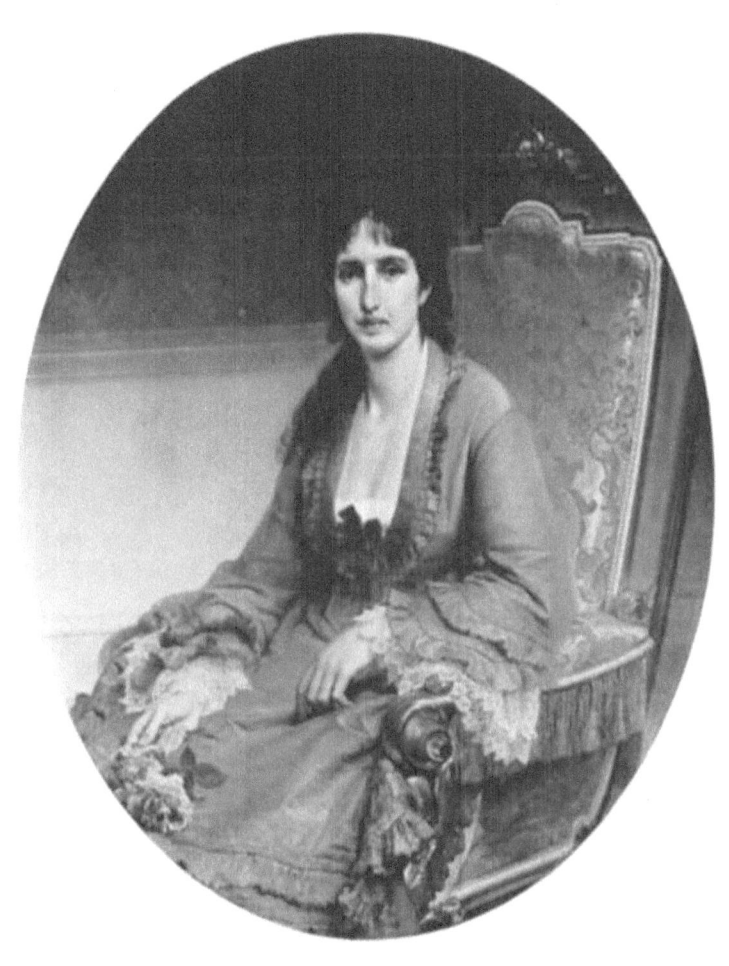

Portrait of Antoniet Negroni Prati Morosini, 1872, Oil
on canvas

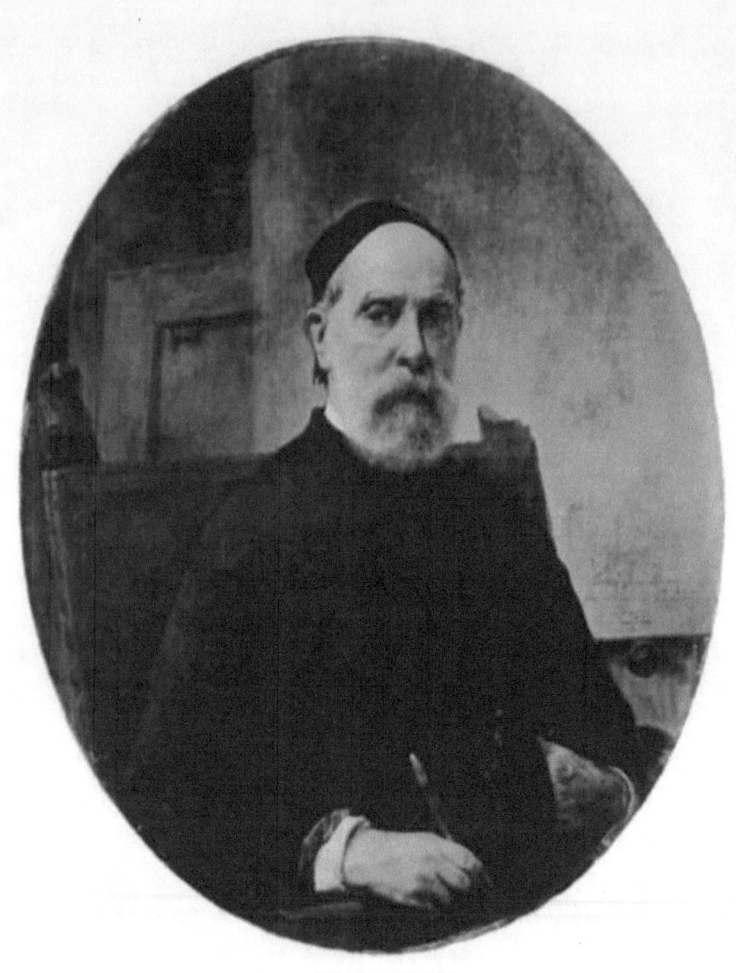

Self Portrait, 1878, Oil on canvas

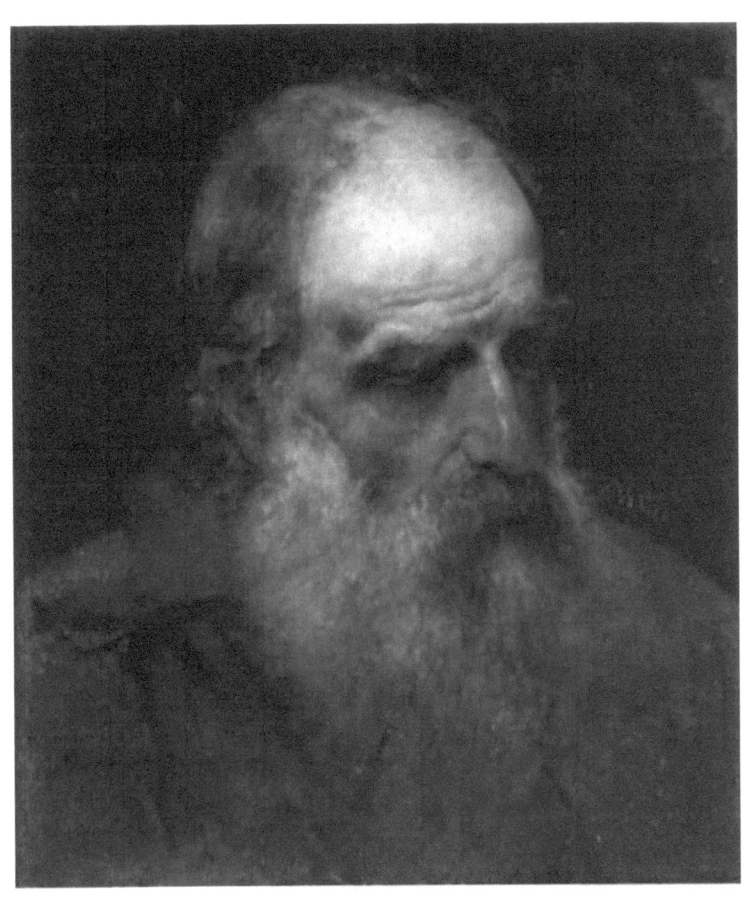

Self-Portrait, 1878, Oil on canvas

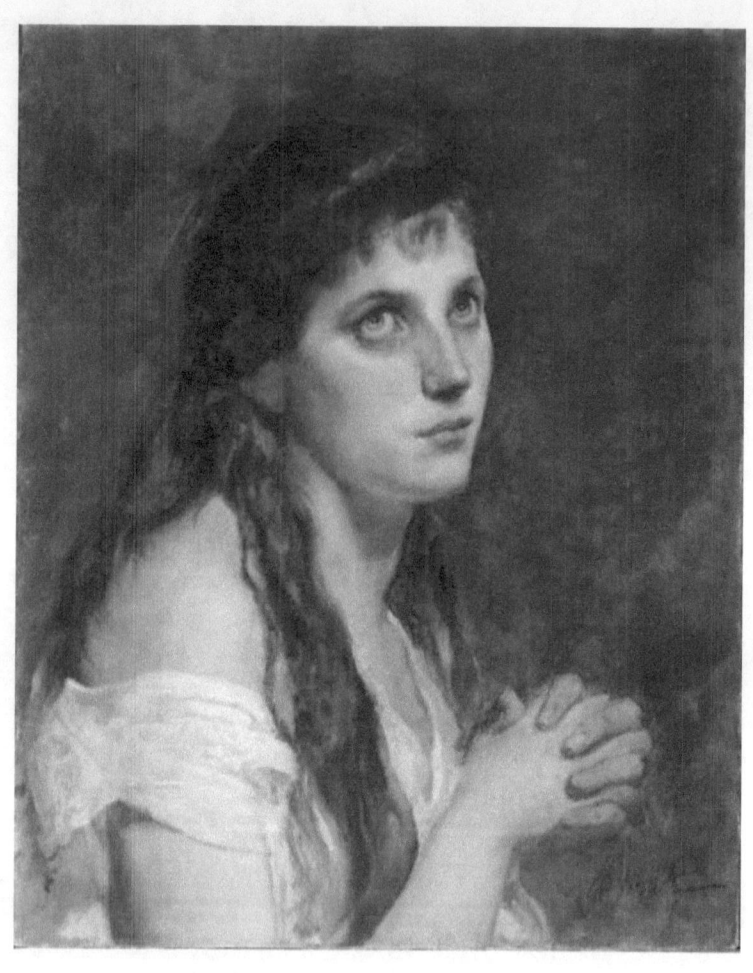

Girl with folded hands, 1880, Oil on canvas

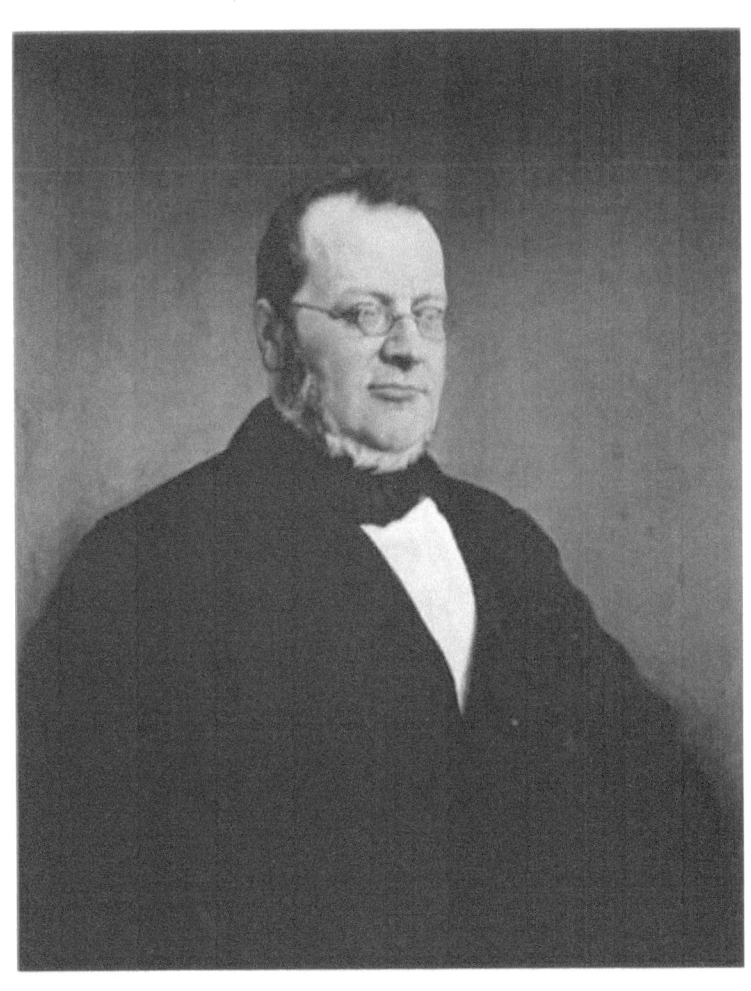

Count Camillo Cavour, Oil on canvas

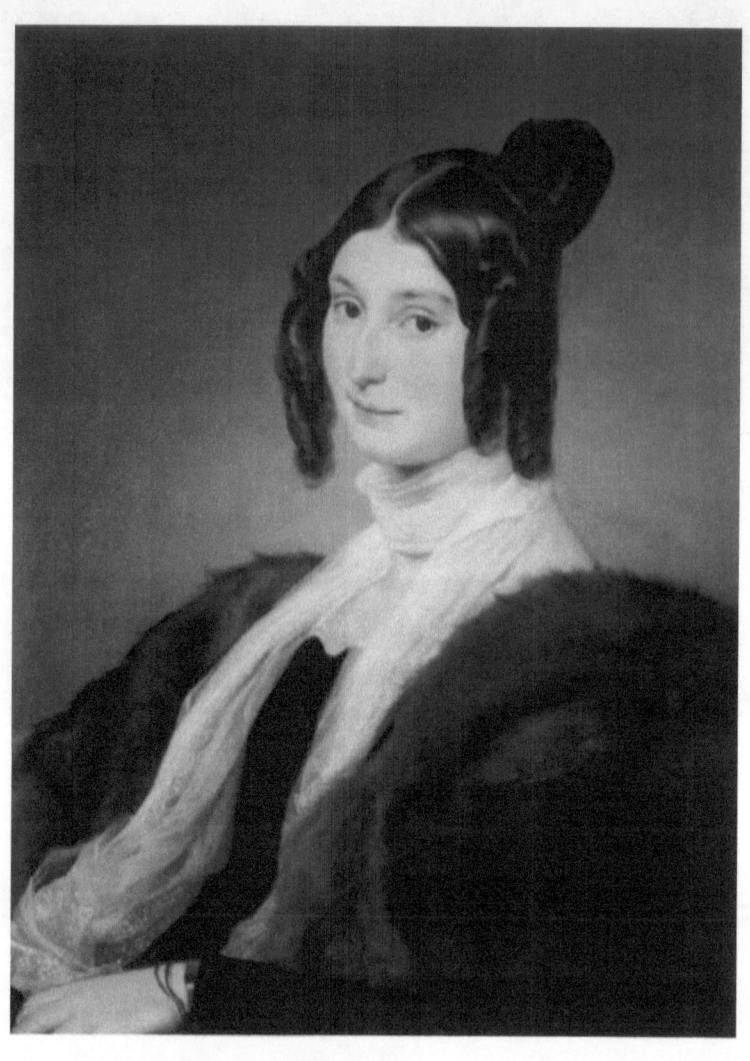

Portrait of Clara Maffei, Oil on canvas

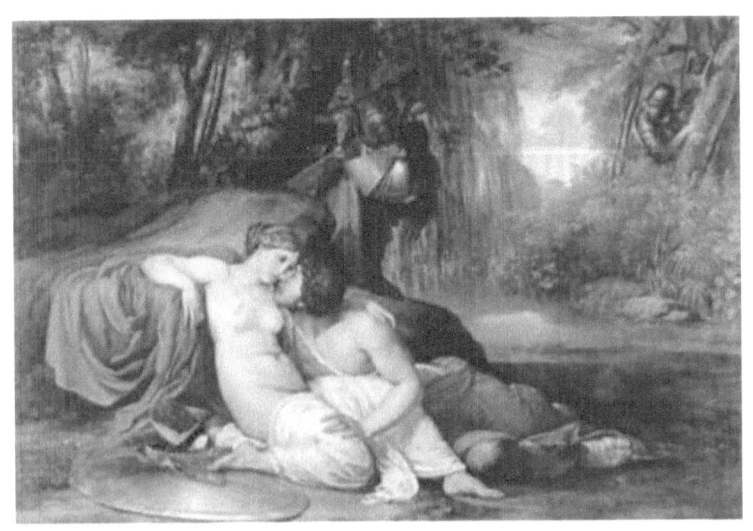

Rinaldo and Armida, Oil on canvas

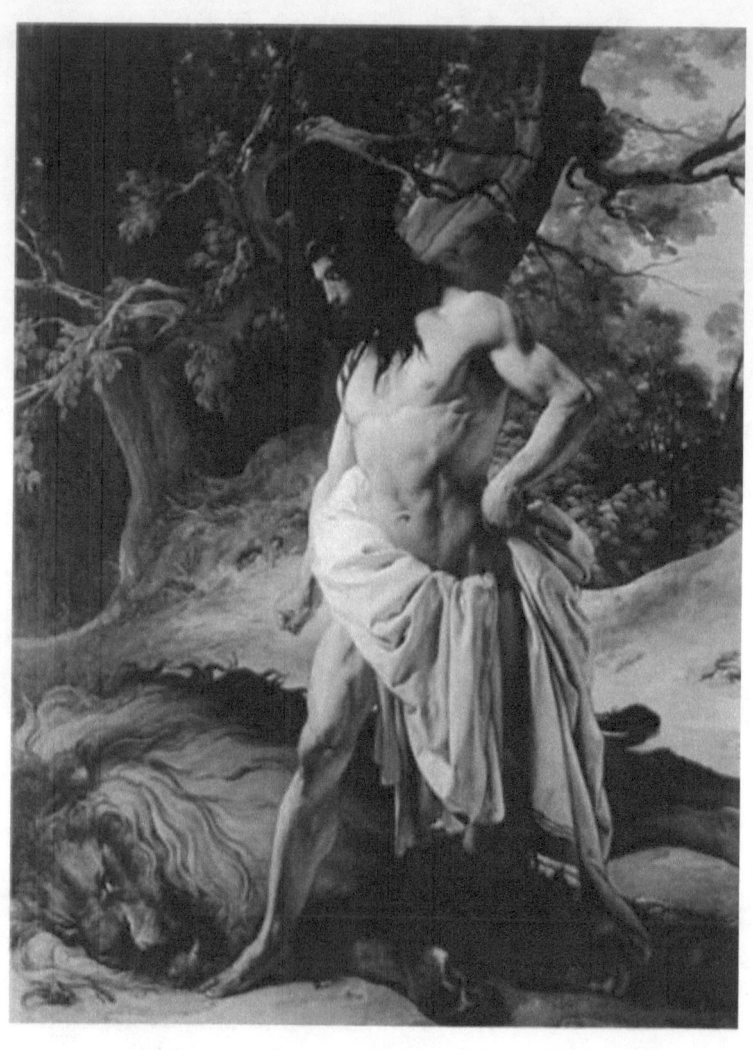

Samson Slays the Lion, Oil on canvas

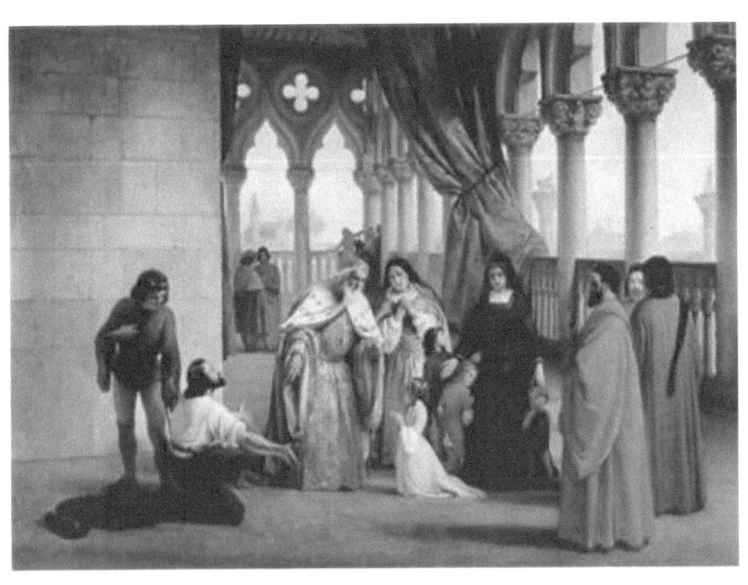

-

The Two Foscari: Francesco Foscari, Doge of Venice
and his family, Oil on canvas

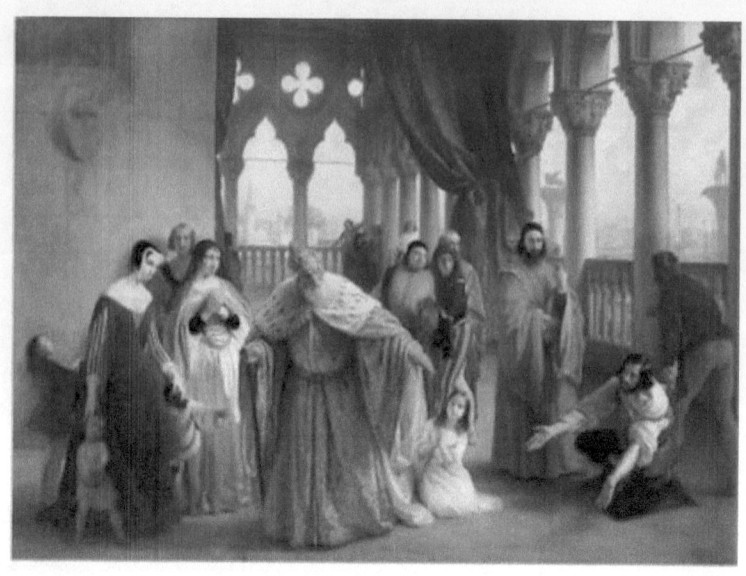

The Last Meeting between Jacopo Foscari and his
Family before Being Sent into Exile, Oil on canvas

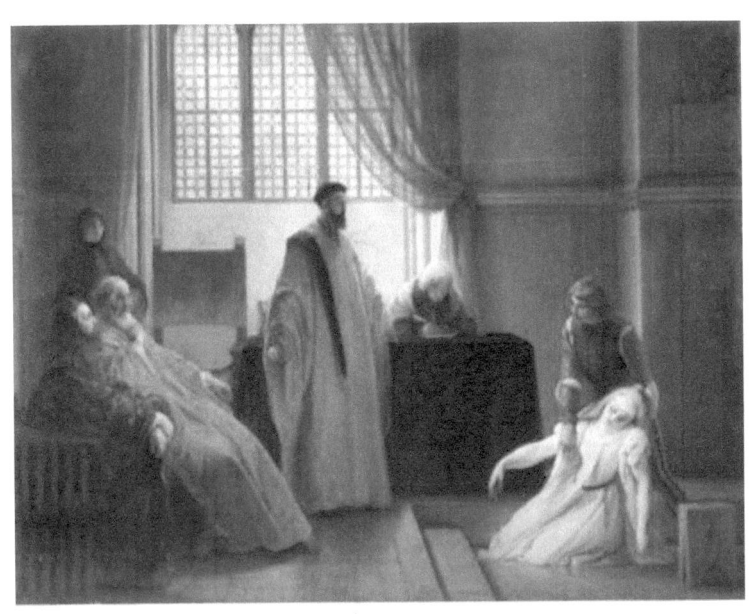

Valenza Gradenigo before the Inquisitor, Oil on canvas

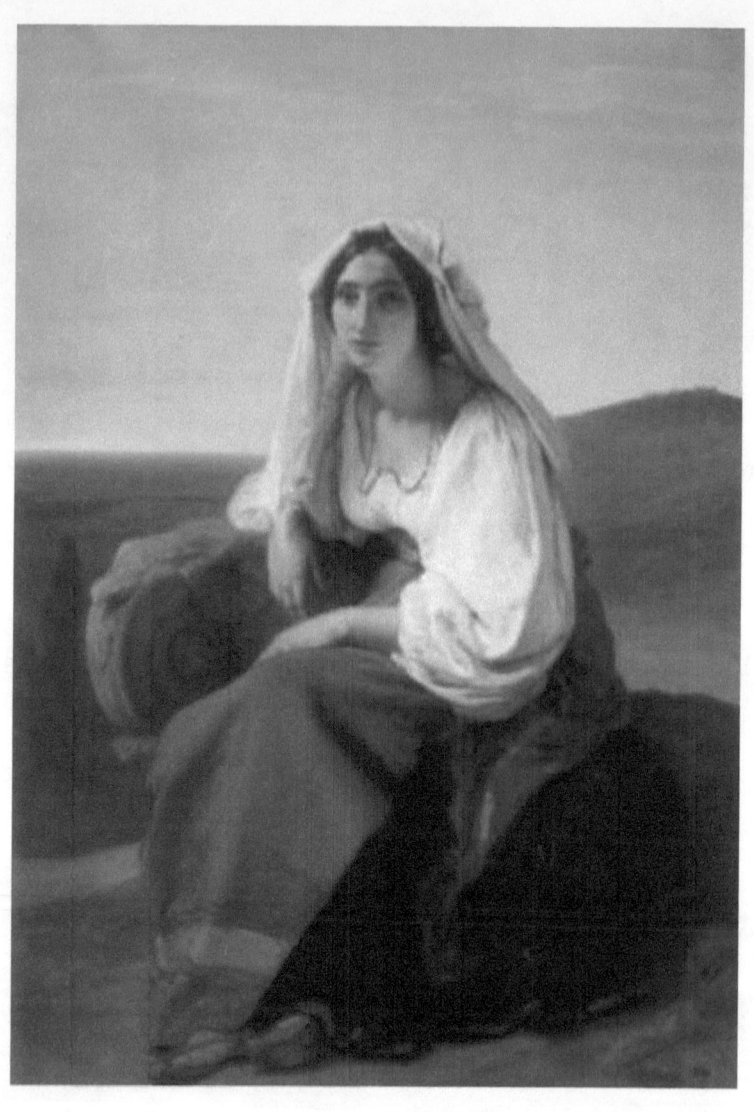

La Ciociara, Oil on canvas

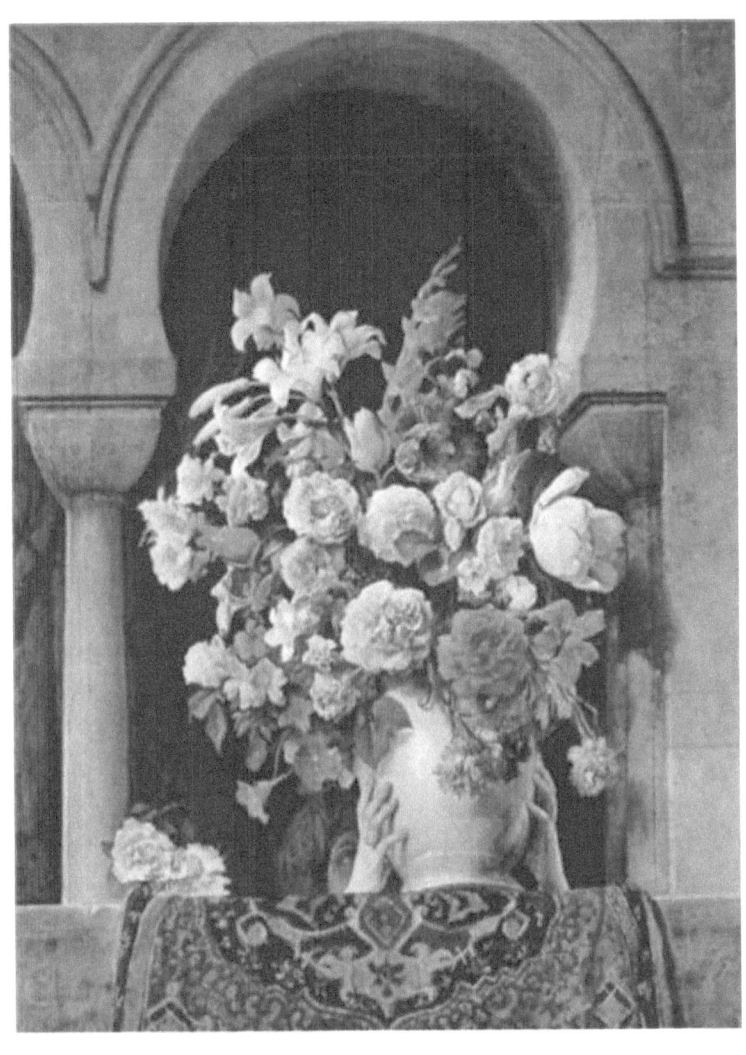

Vase of Flowers on the Window of a Harem, Oil on canvas

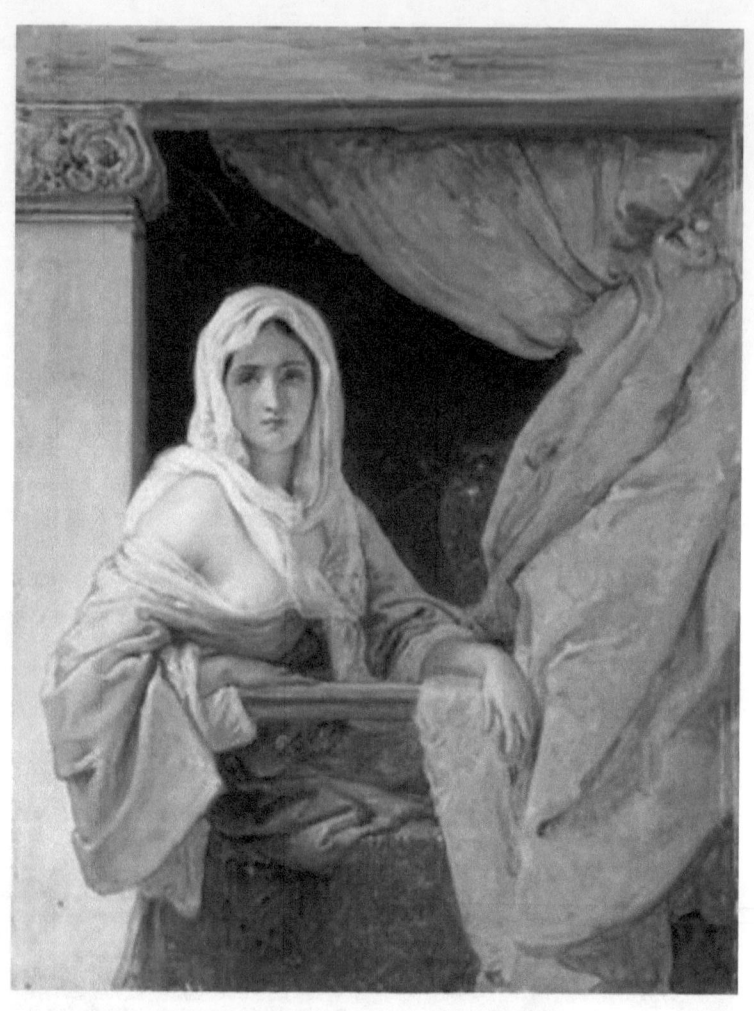

Odalisca, Oil on cartboard